Encounters
With Authors

Other books by Ian Young:

Sex Magick

The Stonewall Experiment:
A Gay Psychohistory

Out In Paperback:
A Visual History of Gay Pulps

The AIDS Cult:
Essays on the Gay Health Crisis
(ed. with John Lauritsen)

The AIDS Dissidents:
An Annotated Bibliography

The AIDS Dissidents 1993-2000:
A Supplement to the Annotated Bibliography

Encounters With Authors

Essays on
Scott Symons
Robin Hardy
Norman Elder

by
Ian Young

SYKES PRESS

SYKES PRESS
2483 Gerrard St. East
Toronto, Canada M1N 1W7

Distributed in Canada by:
Ian Young Books
2483 Gerrard St. E.
Toronto, ON M1N 1W7 Canada
ianyoungbooks.com

Distributed in USA by:
Sibling Rivalry Press
13913 Magnolia Glen Dr.
Alexander, AR 72002, USA
siblingrivalrypress.com

First edition 2013

LIBRARY AND ARCHIVES CANADA CATALOGUING IN PUBLICATION

Ian Young, 1945 -
    Encounters with Authors: Scott Symons, Robin Hardy, Norman Elder /
    by Ian Young
    1st ed.

ISBN 978-0-9695286-2-3
    1. Symons, Scott, 1933 - 2009. 2. Hardy, Robin, 1964 - 2001. 3. Elder,
    Norman, 1939 - 2003.
    I. Young, Ian, 1945 - II. Title.

Cover design by Mona Z. Kraculdy
Cover art by Nichola Battilana, from a photograph of Norman
    Elder and Henry the Pig (photographer unknown)
Photo of Scott Symons p. 11 by John S. Gray
Printed in Canada by Coach House Printing

For my old friends

Table of Contents

Introduction and Acknowledgements

The only time I ever met that iconic - and iconoclastic - figure Quentin Crisp, I was walking down Second Avenue in Manhattan and he was a few steps ahead of me. I realized who it was: the neckerchief, the broad-brimmed hat, the determined walk–who else could it be? Suddenly from across the avenue, a bare-headed man in a brown overcoat darted through the traffic and headed rapidly toward us. He rushed up to Quentin Crisp, grabbed the hat from his head, threw it to the sidewalk with a rough flourish, and ran off. As I stepped into the cloud of dust stirred up by the very stylish hat, its owner, a few steps ahead of me, had just realized he was suddenly hatless. I picked up the hat, dusted it off, and handed it to him.

"*Thank* you!" he said.

My brief encounter with Quentin Crisp occurred, appropriately enough, on the street. But over several decades as a writer, anthologist and sometime publisher, I have had occasion to meet a variety of authors from several countries. I find myself particularly drawn to artists whose individualism led them to follow their own distinctive paths, regardless of categories or expectations–men like Oswell Blakeston, Wallace Hamilton, Kenneth Hopkins, Jonathan Williams and Kirby Congdon. The three essays collected here are my reminiscences of three such idiosyncratic authors: Scott Symons, Robin Hardy, and Norman Elder.

Scott was the grandson of the redoubtable William Perkins Bull, the so-called "Duke of Rosedale" in the days when wealthy Torontonians could still imagine themselves to be colonial nobility. Like Verlaine, he fled respectability for... just exactly *what* would be the question dogging the remainder of his life. He embarked on - and either abandoned or sabotaged - several brilliant careers before publishing a series of "novels" composed essentially of fictional reworkings of his own fate.

Robin was a young writer, trained in law, who emerged as a journalist at *The Body Politic,* the radical gay newsmagazine based in Toronto. He became an activist for the gay cause, then still struggling in the courts and on the streets. He died suddenly and accidentally in his mid-thirties, leaving unfinished his book on the ideals of gay liberation and their fate in the age of AIDS.

Norman did not consider himself a writer at all, but rather a traveller, collector and amateur explorer. Newspapers compared him to Doctor

Doolittle, Gerald Durrell and Indiana Jones. A classically eccentric gentle-man-adventurer, he appeared oddly out of place in what was still, for all its vaunted transformation, "Toronto the Good."

These three were friends of mine, significant people in my life. All three were native-born "Anglo" Canadians at a time when Canada was still finding its voice and the national identity was going through one of its periodic renewals. All three were homosexuals when homosexuality was emerging, rapidly and unsteadily, from stigma and criminality to uneasy acceptance. All three were born under the sign of Cancer—moody, imaginative, and tenacious.

I wrote these pieces because I wanted to memorialize my friends by conveying something of their personalities, their achievements, and the impressions they made—on me and on the others around them. As it happens, their stories raise a number of intriguing questions, on subjects from the pitfalls of patronage to the peculiarity of omens, from our treatment of animals to the social psychology of illness. I offer them as fragmentary accounts of three extraordinary lives which—like any life—may be in danger of being forgotten.

I would like to express my thanks to my partner Wulf, for all his assistance, and to the following people who generously shared their thoughts, memories and records with me: Scott Bell, Conrad Black, Sandy Busby, John Robert Colombo, Andrew D'Cruz at *Toronto Life*, Anne Dondertman and the staff of the Thomas Fisher Rare Book Library, James Dubro, Kathy Frost, Robert Fulford, Hamish Grant, John S. Gray, John Haddad, Eloise Hardy, Michael Higgins, David Mason, John McConnell, Grant Macleod, Don McLeod, Guy Nokes, Frank Ogden, Ralph Reppert, Duane Robertson, Jeffrey Round, Nik Sheehan, Paul Trollope, Bill Young, the late John Grube and the late Bill Jamieson, as well as others who wish to remain anonymous. Special thanks to Bryan Borland and Jerry Rosco.

I would also like to thank John Metcalf, Daniel Wells and Alex Good of *CNQ: Canadian Notes & Queries*, where "A Whiff of the Monster: Encounters with Scott Symons" and "The Trials of Norman Elder" were first published.

For the record, both Quentin Crisp and I were born under the sign of Capricorn.

A Whiff of the Monster:
Encounters with Scott Symons

"I certainly am 'a legend in my own time' in Canada...I am also a Canadian of formidable cultural background and education. And eloquent." - Scott Symons

"He was a catalyst for changing the fabric of society. He tells the truth."
                                                    - Donald Martin

"A negative catalyst going through life on autopilot" - Dennis Lee

"A genius without talent" - John Robert Colombo

"I'll be the organ grinder and you can be the monkeys."
                                                    - Scott Symons

"That's a *hell* of a letter to send to *me!*"
The loud voice over the phone—angry, male, *tremolo*—had woken me from an afternoon nap, and whoever it was had not announced himself. As I mumbled "Who's this?" into the receiver, I realized the caller was—*had* to be—Scott Symons, 38-year old *enfant terrible* of the Toronto literary scene circa 1971. He was shouting at me from the Bracebridge monastery to which he habitually retreated. I had written Scott a letter he didn't like. And now there would be a price to pay because as Scott said—and this was not the only time he is reported to have said it—*"no one fucks with Scott Symons and gets away with it!"*

I had met Scott Symons four years earlier when a mutual interest in Allen Ginsberg brought us both to Toronto's Convocation Hall in 1967, the year of the nation's Centennial and the legendary Summer of Love. Canada's hundredth year as a nation had a particularly liberating effect on the young, who experienced it as not only a watershed in the country's history and outlook, but a long-awaited national coming of age, the occasion marked by Expo 67, an extravagant World's Fair in Montreal.

A cultural breakthrough begun in the early Sixties with the emergence of a new crop of artists, writers and publishing houses, coincided with the rise of the hippie movement and the emergence of a national leader of a new sort—Pierre Elliot Trudeau. By 1967, Canada's Flower Children were being uprooted, shaken loose and scattered across the nation, and the streets and cafés of Toronto's Yorkville bohemia had become fertile ground for artists and restive youth from across the country. I was a 22 years old college student with a handful of verses published in two little magazines. One was called *One*; it was a discreet, rather obscure American periodical for homosexuals. The other was the once-staid Victoria College literary journal *Acta Victoriana*. *Acta* was published from a one-room cellar with an inconspicuous entrance half-hidden by a well-manicured lawn. It was a cut above the average college lit mag, being both attractive and readable. The student staff were an astonishingly talented - and handsome - lot and included three future Governor General's Award Winners, David Gilmour, Greg Hollingshead and John Ayre, future biographer of Vic's preeminent intellectual Northrop Frye. Next door at the theatre space, Ayre's playwright friend Graham Jackson was causing a *frisson* of excitement. With his luminous eyes, luxuriant curls and a slight limp that gave him a Byronic swagger, Graham turned heads just by entering a room.

While the student writers edited *Acta*, Vic's faculty included Frye himself and poets Dennis Lee, David Knight, Francis Sparshott and Frye's disciple and rumoured paramour (there were whispers of a secret passage behind the bookshelves) the imperious Jay MacPherson. In her quarters, Dr. MacPherson presided over her own chilly poetry salon, dispensing literary formulae like castor oil.

The poems I published at Vic seem unexceptionable now but struck Canadian readers of the day as unusually daring. With titles like "The Moth Boy" and "The Skull," they were openly gay in a way that had never been seen in CanLit. In high school I had explored books of a certain tendency, from Plato to Stephen Spender, but in the Sixties, same-sex relationships were just beginning to peek out of the Canadian literary closet. An early breakthrough had come in 1964 when the British house of Secker & Warburg published *The Desert of the Heart*, a novel by the American-born Jane Rule. The first home-grown products came the following year. Edward Lacey's mordant poetry chapbook *The Forms of Loss* became the first openly gay book published in Canada. And John Herbert's rivetting prison drama *Fortune and Men's Eyes* was workshopped at Stratford. Considered far too shocking for Canadians, it failed to find a sponsor until 1967 when it opened off Broadway and became an instant hit.

The year before the much-anticipated Centennial saw the appearance of a brilliant second novel by Leonard Cohen, anointed disciple of the messianic Irving Layton, the man who brought sex to Canada. *Beautiful Losers* had an important gay character, the mysterious soap-collecting separatist referred to only as F, a "hopped-up" radical who dies "in a padded cell, his brain rotted from too much dirty sex." No role models here, but the Sixties were nevertheless bringing rapid changes to Canada. By 1967, the country Frederick Philip Grove thirty years before had called "a non-conductor for any sort of intellectual current" was suddenly effecting cultural electricity. As one observer put it, "everyone's sexuality was bouncing off the walls." Even so, Toronto the Good was not ready for the explosive *succès de scandal* that followed.

Combat Journal for Place d'Armes: A Personal Narrative was released by Canada's leading publishing house McClelland & Stewart at the beginning of 1967 as Scott Symon's Centennial gift to the nation. It was in no way a conventional novel, in that it reclaimed the original meaning of the word novel—*new*. This was something new. The authentic, insistent voice of a delirious Tory renegade who can't stop writing diaries. The "personal narrative" of *Place d'Armes* is an oddly complex journalistic montage. The original hardcover version was ingeniously designed by master printer Stan Bevington to resemble an old-fashioned notebook, complete with attached prints, postcards and fold-out maps —a time-travelling jacket, with big pockets.

Place d'Armes relates the story of a married, well-connected Torontonian named Hugh Anderson, whose life parallels that of his creator. Anderson, an authoritarian elitist in a love-hate relationship with his own class, country and background, rages against a Canadian culture he sees as denying both its British roots and its capacity for sensuous, and sensual, self-expression. Anderson is an avid hater whose targets range from Methodism and William Lyon Mackenzie to the new flag, Expo 67 and various passers-by on the street whose aesthetic sensibilities he longs to whip—literally—into shape.

Hugh Anderson's escape from an emasculated culture he blames for having blocked, perhaps blighted, his power to love involves immersing himself in the life of Montreal's historic Place d'Armes, and having sex with the young hustlers he meets there who "touch him in a way no-one has ever touched him in his own community," presumably because he never made it down Yonge Street as far as the St. Charles Tavern. While recording this pilgrimage in his diary, Anderson is also at work on a novel about a character called Alexander, who is yet another authorial double. Or triple. Unusually for so personal a novelist, Symons writes always in the third person. His fictionalized journals involve a series of near-identical alter egos, each furiously writing about the next. One of them has a Governor General's Award.

A brief excerpt from *Combat Journal for Place d'Armes:*

> *"The gift of insite. That is my battle in La Place. The right to remain open . . . to see . . . to have insite. I must incite insite. And if it is necessary to incite homosexation to propitiate my long rejected insite, then it must be done . . . . If I cannot, then I am dead. But if I do I risk my sanity! . . .*
>
> *"Only this Diary keeps me firmly in 3-D . . . when I am in flight from the disembodiment of 2-D or in pursuit of 4-D. . . 4-D - my unknown birthright, constrained into 3-D, and finally dissolved by 2-D (the proxy plenitude of the positivist priests . . . professorial, psychiatrical, professions).*
>
> *"It involves three different men, moralities, societies . . . visions. Each in irreparable conflict.*
>
> *"In 4-D body is imbedded . . . a world of love.*
> *"In 3-D body is detached . . . world of common-sense.*
> *"In 2-D body is dissolved . . . world of non-sense.*
>
> *"And the Canadian is exposed in a unique immediacy to all three at once. His American heritage is 2-D (the American dream); his British heritage is 3-D (Parliamentarian's Club); his French-Catholic heritage is 4-D (Peasant Baroque!) . . . .*
> *"I become either Protean, or insane!"*

Though the "Personal Narrative" of *Place d'Armes* does include the tangled thread of a plot, its strength is in its spirited, all-out manhandling of the language. Rendered in five different typefaces, it is both playful and enraged (or self-indulgent, depending on your point of view), often over-wrought, and sprinkled with odd barbarisms ("psychiatrical", "parasite" as a verb), useful coinages ("homosentient") and delicious McLuhanish puns like "the hermaphrobike," who could well be a relative of the suicidal Dan-

ish Vibrator in Cohen's *Beautiful Losers*. Its trajectory (Scott's language, I
mean, not the Danish Vibrator, who merely threw himself into the sea) occasionally soars heroically, only to turn abruptly on itself for yet another
vitriolic but pointless—because endlessly repeated—confrontation with Canada, and with the reader. "Expos 67."

The book is full of abusive tantrums; as Mencken sagely observed,
"the public likes to read abuse." Symons harangues the reader in a fictional
language suggestive of a series of experimental, sometimes discordant jazz
riffs, many of which elide and mutate and instead of resolving, feverishly
repeat, eventually disintegrating, or collapsing into themselves. The voice is
strictly solo, but we are treated to some dazzling and spirited improvisa-
tions throughout the gig. It is Scott Symons'—and Hugh Anderson's—wild
verbal probes that provide inspired comic relief to *Place d'Armes*, without
which it would be intolerable, and probably unreadable.

Scott Symons and his protagonist were not the first Anglo-Saxons
to slough off their past, heal their psychic wounds and warm their cockles
by consorting with prostitutes in less Protestant climes. But Symons,
award-winning journalist, Rosedale elitist, scion of the establishment, delivered his message from the sexual—and political—front lines in nearby
French Canada. It was brave, personal, "homosentient," and enormously
angry, and English Canada was quite shaken by it. The fact that Symons
was no stray dog but "the pedigreed son of a Rosedale bitch" made his
barking-mad dash for freedom all the more unlikely, and unseemly. And
shocking.

The dichotomy between Scott's attitude and his background - and
his ambivalence about both - were highlighted by the pair of contrasting
author's photos on the paperback edition of *Place d'Armes*. On the front
cover Scott is dressed with casual ease in a duffle-coat and sneakers. On
the back, a formal portrait by Ashley and Crippen has him brooding with
hand on brow, wearing a cravat. These images were reflected by two match-
ing, or rather unmatching, descriptive blurbs, one printed above the other.
The first could only have been written by Scott, or someone channelling
him: it emphasizes the *Combat Journal* as an all-out "assault" on its
"target"—an urban environment in which nothing is what it purports to be.
It concludes: "As (Hugh Anderson) discovers that these buildings are people, places, himself, multidimensioned, he loses his mind, becomes a fig-
ment of the imagination of La Place d'Armes, keeps encountering predato-
rial denizens, Blondebeestes, Royal Canadian Commissars, is saved only by
an enactment which destroys his male maidenhead forever and relentlessly
resurrected arraigns all Montreal before him—whip-bitch, federaste[1], Expos
67—invulnerable accusation, then turns and plunges into La Place to complete his mission by giving Body and Blood." Whew! And that was just the
blurb!

---

1. *Federaste* or *féderaste*, a conflation of "féderaliste" and "pédéraste," was a coinage of Quebec
    separatists alluding to the alleged sexual proclivities of their federalist opponents, particu-
    larly Pierre Elliot Trudeau.

This was Symons in full bandolier-bedecked combat fatigues. And there was more to come. Underneath, prominently placed but in smaller type, was set out a different set of credentials. A sober recital that could have been cribbed from *Who's Who* paraded the insurgent's august ancestors, his degrees from Cambridge and the Sorbonne, his National Newspaper Award, his prestigious curatorial positions, his visiting professorship, his consultancy at the Smithsonian. Curiously, no mention of that old standby of the respectable author: the wife. But clearly, Scott Symons wanted it known that he was not just any old rebel off the street, or la Place. He was *somebody*.

Specifically, he was the maternal grandson of the legendary William Perkins Bull, the wealthy Toronto eccentric known as "the Duke of Rosedale." Bull, an oil and lumber baron, was a historian, naturalist and philanthropist, adviser to Prime Ministers Laurier and Borden, prominent Freemason, and personal attorney of department store magnate Timothy Eaton. He published an array of books said to have been written largely by his stable of researchers. His daughter, Scott's mother, was known in Rosedale as "the Pink Lady," not for her politics which were quite conventional, but for the powerful cocktails she served her guests.

Despite his establishment background, Symons proclaimed, "My heart is Québecois!" Yet his novelistic view of his Montreal sexual experiences is as deeply ambiguous as the rest of his feelings. Hugh Anderson is seen as "hell-bent for heaven... sainting for sinhood.... To see La Place, to write my novel, to come alive, again, I must fall, utterly. To share my love, I must humiliate me... must grovel. Stand waist deep in the shit... and then sing." This tormented view of sex, sin and sanctity is more Baudelaire/Genet than Whitman/Carpenter. The English poet Kenneth Hopkins quipped that Scott was "waist deep in the shit, crying *Shit!*"

Combat Journal for Place d'Armes records a series of encounters that often seem more martial, or more ceremonial, than amatory. The metaphor of the War of the Sexes is a common, indeed ancient one in heterosexual lore, but is surprisingly rare in gay discourse; there are almost no fights in gay bars. But *Place d'Armes* was precursor to a number of works published during the Gay Liberation period of the Seventies. *The Wild Boys,* William Burroughs' paean to post-pubescent anarchy, appeared in 1971, and John Rechy's *The Sexual Outlaw* in 1977. The young men in *The Wild Boys* are runaways and castaways who employ bizarre weapons and whom society tries, and fails, to destroy; the young men in *The Sexual Outlaw* are depicted as urban front line fighters, shock troops, in a sexual guerilla war against their own society. Their bodies *are* their weapons. The New York gay writer George Whitmore suggested the point of engaging in extreme sex was to be seen to do it "without flinching," i.e. sex as defiance, a courageous proof of one's masculinity. Whitmore's colleague Edmund White suggested that gay men should regard their venereal diseases as badges of honour, like combat medals in a revolutionary sexual war. *Place d'Armes* presented the first of a rising generation not of activists necessarily, but of combative sexual outlaws. What gave rise to them? John Rechy answered with one word: "Rage."

At any rate, it seems evident the outraged, enraged and outrageous chief combat journalist of *Place d'Armes* may well be suffering from acute battle fatigue, not to say shell shock. He seems a man in precarious psychological equilibrium, perhaps in imminent danger of mental collapse. How the author is doing is less certain.

Canadian reviewers recognized the novel's crotchety uniqueness, some taking a not unsympathetic view of its challenge to frosty, thawing Upper Canadian puritanism. But one particular review was to become notorious, and to help make Scott notorious: Robert Fulford's column in the *Toronto Star* was entitled (presumably by a sub-editor) "A monster from Toronto." It was judicious, insightful, and so devastating that Scott was still smarting from it over three decades later and an ocean away.

Fulford's piece began: "The hero of Scott Symons' first novel, *Place d'Armes,* may well be the most repellent single figure in the recent history of Canadian writing." Fulford describes Hugh Anderson as "a monster of snobbishness still wedded to an aesthetic view of life that can be called—depending on the degree of your benevolence—either aristocratic or fascist." Symons, Fulford explains, is "writing a novel about a man who is writing a novel about a man who is writing a novel," each of the novelists being more like Symons than the last. "This is nothing if not ingenious, and it works, but halfway through the book it grows tiresome."

The column went on to describe the book as overwritten as well as overproduced, revealing "more ambition than talent.... The author makes each of his points half a dozen times, and they do not improve through repetition." *Place d'Armes* was characterized as "a kind of higher journalism," (This was the heyday of Tom Wolfe and Hunter S. Thompson). "When it departs from this—when it tries to develop human insights, or tries to convey passion—it fails badly. The hero's problem is that he cannot love; the author's problem is that he can write neither with nor about love."

Symons'—and much of the reading public's—reaction to the *Star's* review focussed on its title. It was the fictional Hugh Anderson, of course, not his creator, who had been accused specifically of loveless monstrosity. But the title stuck. The Monster from Toronto was born. Symons was understandably upset, forgetting in his anger that 1) "All publicity is good publicity," and 2) "If you dish it out, you should be able to take it."

Fulford's column was hardly the first time a Canadian author had been subjected to a journalistic savaging of his or her fictional creation. Three years previously, George Robertson had written in the pages of *Canadian Literature* that the central character of Margaret Laurence's now-classic *The Stone Angel,* was "as unpleasant a heroine as one is likely to meet...proud, bitter, and vengeful...bloated...blind and selfish." (George Robertson, "An Artist's Progress," *Canadian Literature* No. 21, Summer 1964.) Apparently no umbrage was taken on that occasion as Mrs. Laurence did not assume the characterization was necessarily aimed at her.

Symons felt no such distance from his fictional clones. Thus Fulford's verdict was understandably viewed as an unwarranted personal denunciation. When I first met Scott, the furor over his debut novel was still breaking. *Place d'Armes* had been published in January. In February, the University College Literary & Athletic Society at the University of Toronto sponsored a controversial "psychedelic festival" called Perception '67. This encompassed a variety of events including a series of visionary (or disorienting) "Mind Excursion Rooms" and a Saturday night "Happening" at Convocation Hall featuring the music group The Fugs and, as an opening act, Beat poet Allen Ginsberg, who read poems and chanted Buddhist hymns. Psychedelic guru Dr. Timothy Leary had also been invited but the Federal Government had barred him from entering the country, citing a conviction for "drug trafficking" (i.e. transporting marijuana across state lines). At the last minute, the University College Principal, Douglas LePan, announced a strict ban from all college properties of "users or advocates of the drug LSD." "Recently," Principal LePan explained, "a far from negligible number of our students had psychic breakdowns and had to withdraw and enter psychiatric wards." Faced with such disturbing phenomena, LePan's administrative instinct was to suppress, not encourage, discussion. LePan, an author and former diplomat, had been an aide to Lester Pearson. His war novel *The Deserter* scandalously won the 1964 Governor General's Award over *The Stone Angel*. (LePan's fear of bad publicity was seen in a new light when he came out of the closet in 1990 at the age of 76.)

Even without Leary or an official panel on drugs, the mid-winter Happening was a success, with a number of Toronto luminaries in attendance, including Marshall McLuhan sporting a "third eye" in the form of a light-refracting disc strapped to his forehead. I didn't see McLuhan but while engrossed in listening to Ginsberg, I became aware that the man I was staring at, sitting directly across the aisle from me, was someone I recognized as the author of a novel I had just read. I had picked up a copy of *Combat Journal for Place d'Armes* soon after it appeared, and admired its inventive language and unprecedented audacity. After the reading, I introduced myself, had a brief conversation with the author, and wandered off home to think about Ginsberg and Symons. Soon afterwards, Scott left the country in an exodus that was to become notorious.

Before *Place d'Armes* changed everything, Scott Symons was known in both English and French Canada as a prescient, award-winning journalist. His series—in French—forecasting Quebec's Quiet Revolution had won the National Newspaper Award. He was a respectably married man with close ties to the academic world, a pious Anglican who retreated from time to time to a provincial monastery to engage in fervent prayer. Those who knew him on a personal level frequently found him sharp, abrasive, and unpredictable—decidedly not a gentleman or what passed for gentleman among those Scott called (reverently, in a chat with the Queen Mother) "Your Majesty's Royal Americans." He was still a celebrated and eminently respectable figure when he received an invitation to speak to the students of a small private school near Bracebridge, Ontario. It was there that he met the strikingly handsome, seventeen year old John McConnell, the bright, alienated son of a prominent Toronto banker. This was the beginning of the odyssey frequently described since as "running away to Mexico with a teen-age boy"—a notorious tandem flight that in fact never occurred. Later conversations with both Scott and John gave a more accurate, though no less extraordinary, story.

Scott was born on July 13, 1933. After graduating from Trinity College at the University of Toronto, he won a Commonwealth Fellowship to King's College, Cambridge. From there he went to the Sorbonne. The woman he married at the age of 25 was, he often reminded people, the granddaughter of a leading bank president. The marriage had gotten off to a rocky start when Scott's rudely provocative speech disrupted his own wedding, but it lasted for ten years and produced a son, born in Paris while Scott was working in the wine trade.

"So you could have been a French vintner, Scott," I once remarked.

"Maybe I should have been. But while I was in France I met Julien Green."

Julien Green was an American-born writer who lived in France and wrote in French. It was over dinner with Green and his younger lover (whom he later adopted) novelist Eric Jourdan, that Scott's closet doors first became seriously unhinged. Green, as Scott put it, "introduced me to my gay factor"—not through any erotic suggestion but simply by his eyes going "right through me." Photos of Green show him as an attractive man with a good-humoured smile. But Scott experienced Green's gaze rather as E.M. Forster experienced a friendly pat on the bum delivered by the openly gay George Merrill at the cottage he shared with Whitman's disciple Edward Carpenter. "It seemed to go straight through the small of my back into my ideas," Forster recalled, "without involving any thought." The frisson from that touch was the genesis of Forster's classic gay novel *Maurice*.

Julien Green's searching gaze apparently opened up long dormant feelings in Scott. According to Charles Taylor's masterly essay in *Six Journeys: A Canadian Pattern*, Scott, while a young student at Trinity College Schools in Port Hope, had contracted an affair with another boy—an affair that Scott broke off when, believing that "his body and his desires were dirty," he "felt an overwhelming inner veto." Later, Taylor wrote, "he would blame the school, his family and his society for compelling him to suppress his love." Scott apparently came to see this repudiation as "decisive, and crippling." He remained, in his own words "eternal thirteen; eternally the boy reaching out to touch but never being allowed to do so...except as Mommy and Authority permitted." The penetrating look of a French novelist across a Parisian dining table had resurrected these awkward suppressed memories. Nevertheless, Scott and his young wife returned to Canada to live at her wealthy family's Ontario farm, which they purchased with money from Symons' family. And Scott wrote his acclaimed series of articles for *La Presse* on the coming political and social upheaval in Quebec.

"I was saying that Canada was going to explode," Scott told me. "There was going to be a revolution. Trudeau and I became good friends through that. He was editing *Cité Libre* at the time...we had a real symbiotic relationship that we were both aware had a sexual component. We were both aware that the other was homosentient. In those days, no-one said anything about homosexuality. Many of the guys at *La Presse* were gay but you certainly didn't walk up to them and announce it. Of course I was married at the time."

Scott's establishment connections and a wide and discerning knowledge of Canadian antiques paved the way for him to become Curator of Canadiana at Toronto's Royal Ontario Museum, one of a number of positions from which he was dismissed for causing too many problems. About the same time, he told his wife about his growing attraction to men. "She said if you want to do that, you should do it." So he left her in Ontario and headed for Montreal.

Those trips, and his voluminous journals, were, Scott said, his way of knowing himself and expressing himself. "Because you couldn't talk about anything in my culture in those days. You couldn't even talk about heterosexuality. Though the French Canadians were quite a bit looser than we were. But you couldn't announce that you were into cocksucking. It would have ended everything. But I published *Place d'Armes* as my gift to Canada for the Centennial. And that led to the breakup of my marriage. We had no intention of separating. We adored each other," he insisted. "But her parents were so nosey and determined to run her life. Her mother was noted for being a cruel woman."

I reminded him that he had been having an affair with the young John McConnell. He recalled meeting John at Muskoka Lakes College, a private school "for kids whose parents couldn't figure out what to do with them. They were a wealthy family. His father ran (Ontario Premier) John Robarts' ad campaigns. I was on a retreat at the monastery in Bracebridge and was invited to give a talk at the school. After the talk, there was this beautiful boy with flaming red hair, standing in the hall, waiting for me."

Though only seventeen at the time, John was tall and well-built and looked like a lumberjack, which he later briefly became.

"What did you say to him?" I asked.

"Every instinct told me he was profound trouble. I said 'I don't want to talk to you.'"

Scott's answer surprised me. I too had met a beautiful, extraordinary seventeen year old—in a Yorkville sidewalk cafe—and had fallen in love with him. Law or no law, it would never have occurred to me to tell Richard Phelan "I don't want to talk to you." Scott had evidently been conflicted in ways that were foreign to me. But teenage boys can be wilful, and John was not about to be brushed off so easily.

"He had set his sights on me," said Scott, "and he was going to get me. But his parents sent him to a gilded cage in Nassau. I went to San Miguel de Allende in Mexico where I was hanging out with a group of painters including York Wilson and Leonard Brooks. He got a message to me. And I sent him a telegram saying 'Take up your cock and walk.' I remember sitting in the courtyard garden and there he was."

John later confirmed Scott's recollection. So, all later sensational accounts to the contrary, Scott Symons never did "run away to Mexico with a seventeen year old." Nonetheless, John's well-connected father set the police of three countries on the pair, posting a hefty reward for their arrest. When John heard about this, he contacted his sister, asking her to warn their parents that he would kill himself if Scott was jailed. Word soon came back that the reward had been rescinded and that John could pick up his passport at the Canadian embassy. The couple then reentered Canada and fled "to grizzly country" on the Northern BC coast. After various adventures and misadventures there, including a stint at lumberjacking, they resurfaced in Toronto in 1970, where I ran into Scott again.

In the previous year, my longstanding efforts to start a gay organization at the University of Toronto had finally paid off. Whereas before, no-one had dared to come out of the closet, now in the wake of the Stonewall riots in New York and the Trudeau-sponsored decriminalization at home, the situation had suddenly changed. In November of 1969, the first official meeting of the University of Toronto Homophile Association launched what would become the Canadian Gay Liberation movement. When I learned that Canada's best-known gay author was back in town and staying at the Norman Elder Museum and Gallery in Yorkville, I lost no time in dropping by, to ask him to speak to the new group.

By then, Scott's wife, considering herself abandoned, had divorced him, forbidden him ever to see his son again, and sold his property at auction. When I commiserated with Scott about his divorce, he placed the blame squarely upon his in-laws, seeing them as representing an implacably hostile Rosedale establishment of bland, powerful eunuchs and their cruel, unavailable wives. The fact that he had left his wife to live in distant parts with a teenaged lover did not seem to Scott to be grounds for divorce. "The vile cow, doesn't she know how much I love her?"

By my next encounter with Scott, both of us had new books making their way to the store shelves. My poems in *Acta* had been spotted by Dennis Lee, who was about to launch a new publishing company, House of Anansi, with the novelist Dave Godfrey. Dennis asked me for a manuscript, and Anansi published *Year of the Quiet Sun* late in 1969. About the same time, Scott published his second book, an extraordinary production originally called *The Smugly Fucklings*, but after much persuasion released under the more sober title of *Civic Square*.

At 848 pages, *Civic Square: An Original Manuscript by Scott Symons* made *Combat Journal for Place d'Armes* seem concise and coherent. Neither Scott nor his publisher Jack McClelland had relished the daunting task of cutting the idiosyncratic—and ever-expanding—manuscript, and it was recognized that, uncut, it would be, as editor John Robert Colombo later put it, "unmarketable." Scott gave his publishers the same permission he gave the

ORGASM,
CANADA,
and
US....
a public lecture
Scott Symons
- prominent canadian
novelist
thurs. mar. 25   8.p.m.
MEDICAL SCIENCE AUD.
sponsored by the
U of T
Homophile Association.

For Kebir — Marrakshi
And for Tony — Colonel emeritus

and for Ian Young,
homophilissimus!

Scott Symons
July 2006

TOP LEFT: Place d'Armes
(McClelland and Stewart, 1967),
front cover of hardbound edition.

TOP RIGHT: Promotion for Scott's
lecture "Canada, Orgasm and Us",
1971.

LEFT: Helmet of Flesh *(McClelland*
and Stewart, 1986), dedication
page inscribed "and for Ian Young,
homophilissimus! Scott Symons,
July 2006"

surgeon who circumcised his son: "Just take a little bit." The work was eventually issued in a small edition as a Gestetnered typescript of unbound sheets stacked in a large, powder-blue box that simulated the trademark "Birks boxes" of the fashionable Toronto retailers. Each copy of the book was personalized by Scott with distinctive coloured glyphs of fiery, flaming phalli. It remains a controversial work to this day, having been judged (by Patrick Watson) as "extremely skilful" and (by Dennis Lee) as "very badly written."

When I arrived at Norm Elder's Yorkville home and private museum, Scott was sitting on the single bed in his room. He made a gentlemanly pass at me, which I deflected. Scott concluded I must find him "intimidating;" as it happened, I just didn't fancy him. When I moved the conversation to the subject of speaking engagements, Scott said he would be happy to speak to the UTHA and a date was set. We chatted a little about his background, his and his wife's ancestors, and his boyhood at Trinity College Schools, which, knowing my English background, he informed me was "the Canadian Eton."

"I went to Beal," I said, with a certain emphasis. Scott looked at me in silence. Obviously he had never heard of Beal, which was not surprising as it was an undistinguished Ilford grammar school. He shifted his buttocks and emitted a loud and pungent fart and we sat silently, savouring the moment. Scott seemed quite at ease in Norman's quarters, though he later confided that he "didn't sleep comfortably" there because of the pet boa constrictors Norm kept down the hall.

Another young writer who visited Scott around that time was the Lancashire poet Michael Higgins, who was then living in Toronto. When he dropped in on Scott's rooms, Michael was carrying a guidebook to the city of York which he showed Scott, seeing it as an alien but comparable locale to the Place d'Armes. "He snarled with contempt," Michael recalled, "and (literally) threw the book at me, hitting my arm, and saying something along the lines of 'I've been there before, one doesn't need this!'" Michael left thinking Scott to be uncouth as well as over-rated. He never finished reading *Place d'Armes*.

Other meetings were more successful. Scott enjoyed brief liaisons with several UTHA members. The young gay activist Michael Pearl told Scott, after an erotic encounter, "You're a cute old number!" Scott met more formally with our little gay organization more than once in the months that followed, sometimes accompanied by John McConnell. He spoke about their relationship, and about modern civilization's rising competence and declining compassion. He felt Canada was an anaphrodisiac society with a crippling fear of tenderness. He found at the UTHA "a level of intimacy and honesty in discussion," but felt that more should be said about "the nature of a good and deep and extended relationship between two guys—all the difficulties of being a homosentient person in this society." He told the group how both he and John had come from wealthy Toronto homes and, "desperate for love and affection, had to knock down just about every barrier that exists in the Protestant society book to reach out and touch each other." A favourite topic was "the amount of hate" existing not only in society in general but specifically in "the failure to touch" existing in the middle class marriage: what he called "the hate space."

Scott celebrated "the guerilla warfare of the new sensibility," comparing himself to Che Guevara, an insurgent bedecked with explosives. He found much to enjoy in the emerging gay world, but was shocked by the amount of hate he found there. What the gay world had not done successfully, he felt, was putting men "in touch with each other on a long term basis very intimately very relaxedly." He found—and I saw this as quite perceptive—that in both heterosexual and homosexual relationships, "you (often) turn onto somebody, and then when he or she gets close to you, cut him or her off. That was the control system." Scott called this "the negative orgasm cycle." He and John, he told us, were trying to overcome this unhappy situation, and it was "a long, hard trip...the big battle. And it's a battle the whole of our society is in."

By that point, Scott and John had spent some time living in a remote part of Newfoundland, thanks to the first of a series of cash subsidies organized by Scott's friend and patron Charles Taylor, writer son of the millionaire horse breeder E.P. Taylor. (At one UTHA get-together Scott had proudly displayed on a table-top a small stack of high-denomination banknotes, spread into a fan like a hand of playing cards.) The couple had been welcomed by the rural islanders and the motherly Ma Snook. Scott came to admire the locals' "quick responses" and "eyes that look straight into you, as if probing your beauty...constantly alert and aware...fresh and clean inside themselves, like the sea on a calm sunny day." And, he found, they were men and women "honest about their sex. There is none of the morbid division between their desires and their values so true on the mainland... They celebrate in their flesh, and it is beautiful." Nevertheless, at least one woman friend there was offended at what she presumed was Scott's "seduction of a gracious, inexperienced young boy." In fact, John had been sexually active with men for over a year prior to their meeting and had been earnestly looking for an older male partner.

At the UTHA, Scott and John both spoke eloquently, and Scott quickly began to attract a personal following from among the (mostly male) members. He readily agreed to be a speaker at one of the series of public lectures the Association was sponsoring on campus. So it was that on March 25, 1971, in the university's Medical Auditorium, Scott gave a presentation advertised under the title "Canada, Orgasm and Us."

The lecture drew a considerable crowd. Scott talked of his stay in "a falling down goat house about a hundred miles up the coast" from Vancouver, and his life in Newfoundland, "tougher in its climate...it has the wonderful addition of a people and a culture four centuries old." He delighted the audience by declaiming the "Cocks are beautiful...Cocks are Holy Rood" passage from the beginning of *Civic Square*. At one point, departing from his scripted remarks, he began to read a love letter, apparently delivered that very morning from John, who was still back in Trout River, Newfoundland. Scott then removed from the same envelope a nude photo of John which he held aloft and proceeded to circulate around the auditorium. As the lecture continued, the picture of the handsome, naked young man was passed, somewhat nervously, from hand to hand. I was sitting toward the front of the auditorium, on the aisle, and eventually the photo reached me, slightly soiled from having been dropped on the floor. The seats in front of me were empty, everyone was paying attention to Scott, and seeing no outstretched hand, I pocketed the photo to return it after the lecture. As it happened, Scott left quickly with a sizable entourage before I could reach him.

Though radical in some things, I was conservative in others. I had enjoyed hearing of Allen Ginsberg's public disrobings (on being asked "What do you mean by naked?" he had taken his clothes off to demonstrate) but it seemed to me that nude photographs of one's lover should be for private viewing or shared with a few close friends. Passing them through hundreds of sweaty fingers in a public stadium did not strike me as a great idea; displaying one's own nakedness in public is one thing, displaying someone else's, a quite different matter. I doubted it would help Scott's reputation, and if he was going to be the mutinous messiah of the new Canadian gay movement, as was beginning to appear likely, I felt there might well be dangers ahead if he didn't rethink this particular tactic.

As Scott had left for his monastery the morning after the lecture, I wrote him a brief letter suggesting he might want to rethink his approach. Before mailing the note, I thought I should seek a second opinion. I showed it to Paul Pearce, a level-headed member of the UTHA whose judgement I trusted. As he was equally skeptical of Scott's public manner, the letter went in the post the next day, with John's photo enclosed. A couple of days later, I awoke to Scott's challenging voice from the cloister.

One of the duties and prerogatives of friendship is surely to warn of possible dangers ahead, to restrain, to urge caution and reflection. Just in case. This can cause problems, and Scott was not the first, or the last, acquaintance to excommunicate me. My letter on that occasion, if not impertinent, was certainly presumptuous, in that it was a letter that only a friend should write. I had presumed friendship where none really existed, and my little message must have sounded self-righteous, censorious, annoying. As his reaction to *The Star*'s review had shown, Scott was easily rattled when not taken at his own valuation.

By this point, Richard Phelan, the schoolboy I had met during the Summer of Love four years earlier was now a world-travelling student of Buddhism. He had returned to Toronto for a stretch and he and I were hanging out together, collaborating on a book to be illustrated with his drawings. Richard had met both Scott and John and though he may not have been at the "Orgasm" lecture, he certainly had heard about it. Richard was one of those people who never speak ill of anyone, and his only remark on the lecture was "There's a difference between a ballet and a striptease!" But he could tell that Scott's phone call had upset me more than I let on, and once Scott was back in town from his retreat, Rick arranged to visit Scott to see if he could smooth things over.

According to Rick, Scott had been in no mood for tea and *tête à tête*, pressing instead for a more carnal engagement, "All he wanted to do was have sex with me," Richard said with a shrug and a smile. When he demurred, he was accused of having "forgotten how to *celebrate*," which was Scott's word for fuck. "You've been in the *city* too long!" Scott scolded, unaware of Rick's recent wanderings in the far-flung holy places. Realizing his cause was hopeless, Richard gracefully retreated. And that was that. Scott seems never again to have talked to a gay group or associated himself with a gay cause. His brief career as a public spokesman for Gay Lib was over. The next time Scott and I spoke, well over thirty years had passed, Richard was dead, and Scott had returned from his long, self-imposed exile for the last time.

John left Scott in the summer of 1972, shortly after the publication of *Heritage*, Scott's learned, idiosyncratic "furniture novel" (*Heritage: A Romantic Look at Early Canadian Furniture*, McClelland & Stewart, 1971). "We were in a sixteen foot trailer near Trout River Pond," he told me years later. John, who had dropped out of Grade Twelve, had expressed his desire to get a university education. "Working in lumber camps and fisheries was fine for my youth but wouldn't work for me as I aged. I needed to go back and complete my schooling and Scott could not abide that. He wanted me forever young and all for himself—including all of my future." Also complicating things was John's growing interest in homoerotic S/M. John's interests, both erotic and educational, Scott interpreted as rejection, and he responded with a series of verbal assaults.

"When I told Scott I was going to leave him," John wrote, "he exploded into a rant and wouldn't calm down. I told him I was going for a walk." Scott followed John along the lakefront, tackled him, and attacked him, leaving him with a black eye. At that point, John realized he wanted to leave Scott but feared that "if I didn't hold open the possibility of living together he would become violent again." With talk of a trial separation, Scott left for Mexico, and the prospect of renewing his relationship with a woman both he and John had been involved with on a previous trip. "When Scott arrived in Mexico he found that the woman had already moved in with another man. That stirred him to make overtures about getting back together with me."

Scott attributed John's diminishing erotic interest to the pernicious influence of the "squares and smuglies," John told me. "Nothing to do with his big belly." John also began expressing an interest in exploring heterosexual relationships, partly as a way of blocking the possibility of Scott's return. "I wanted to distance myself from him far enough," he recalled, "to make impossible the resumption of our erotic relationship. Going straight served that function." Scott, of course, saw the breakup in a different light, claiming that John had been attempting to kill him by murdering their love. He interpreted John's interests not as the natural feelings and ambitions of an intelligent young man but instead as treachery and attempted homicide. He was persuaded to see a psychiatrist, who told him John was trying to exorcise his own demons (as it were) by projecting them onto Scott. In willing Scott's death, he was absolving himself of the need to commit suicide; he had been exercising a kind of "psychic voodoo." Scott's journals of this period contain many mentions of psychic voodoo, black magic and sadomasochism. He was deeply troubled about his future—and his reputation. "I can't stop him," he wrote in his journal. "And a whole nation will applaud his honesty, his decency, and pay him well..."

After his split with Scott, I continued to see John from time to time until he graduated and left the country. I remember visiting him in his small, cozy apartment near High Park when he was a university student. He told me Scott had sometimes come to see him. On one occasion, after Scott had left, John noticed he had lifted a stack of photos of their time together. Recalling their final meeting, John remembered Scott had showed up "in full leather regalia, harness, boots, leather jacket and Master's cap." They talked briefly and were soon in bed together. Scott took his belt to John. Then, with John still naked on the bed, "Scott abruptly buckled up, suddenly exiting and leaving the apartment door wide open, screaming 'Evil! Evil! Evil!' as he strode down the hall." John never saw Scott again. He started a new life in California, where he became a therapist and a prominent member of the gay leather community.

Scott now saw himself as "a murdered man." By 1973, he had left Canada, recapitulating an earlier stay in Morocco by settling in a well-appointed compound in Essaouira, where he lived for most of the next three decades, leaving the hefty manuscript of his three-part novel *Helmet of Flesh* with Dennis Lee, who spent the next fourteen years shaping it into publishable form. Essaouira seems to have been a favourite spot for Canadian (and other) expatriates. Richard Phelan wrote to me from there in 1972, and in '78, Edward Lacey was arrested for smoking hash in one of the local cafés, jailed for two months, and deported to Spain - an incident Scott regretted not knowing about until much later.

In 1977, Charles Taylor published his book *Six Journeys: A Canadian Pattern*, a collection of sympathetic biographical sketches of Scott and five others who "followed a lonely path in search of a more sustaining vision than was offered by...Canadian society," exploring other cultures and "traditions which modern Canada seeks to denigrate." Taylor quotes Scott's belief that "the Canadian Identity is evil. I am dedicated to the total destruction of the Canadian state." What he anticipated as a replacement is not recorded.

That year, Scott published a lengthy article in a Canadian literary journal entitled "The Canadian Bestiary: Ongoing Literary Depravity" (*West Coast Review*, Vol. 11, No. 3). It is an extended personal reaction to Marion Engel's 1976 novel *Bear,* an odd tale of an unhappy woman who, as Scott puts it, "seduces a poor, tatty bear." Scott was evidently deeply offended by Engel's mildly controversial novel, which confirmed and deepened his convictions about what he saw as the loathsome degeneration of English-Canadian culture. Writing the piece, he confided, his "two central feelings were scorn and outrage."

After a page or so of nervous clowning around, "A Canadian Bestiary" developed into a slashing verbal assault on *Bear* and its author. Feeling the book had been praised for all the wrong reasons, Scott obviously enjoyed venting his indignation. His point was not so much that *Bear* was an over-praised and pretentious book, rather that its very publication and acceptance exemplified the nation's smug, subcultural tawdriness, thus preventing the future publication of other, better books.

His swashbuckling assault having bloodied Ms. Engel and her *Bear,* Scott then mounted a scattershot attack on much of the rest of CanLit. By the end of his thirteen pages, he had savaged not only Ms. Engel ("common...culturally pretentious...with absolutely nothing to say") and her *Bear* ("spiritual gangrene...a Faustian compact with the Devil") but also Irving Layton ("a runt"), Robertson Davies ("Humbug!"), Mordecai Richler ("second rate"), Victor Coleman ("insidiously trivial"), Jacques Godbout ("a federaste"), literary immigrants ("born in Baghdad or Bongo Bongo") and even the Symons-friendly Coach House Press ("ghoulish...psychedelic masochismo"), not to mention his old nemesis Robert Fulford ("Bobo Fullblown").

In this extraordinary one-man uprising against CanLit, the only writers to emerge more-or-less unscathed are the two ageing doyennes Margaret Laurence and Marie-Claire Blais; Dennis Lee, then in the initial throes of sculpting Scott's monumental *Helmet of Flesh*; and one or two lesser-known figures who are damned with faint praise. The essay finishes with a disdainful denunciation of "the literature of depravity and psychic deprivation," and a ready prophecy that the next "with-it-lit" fad will be "sado-masochistic homosexuality!" which Symons characterizes, obscurely, as a "natural kick-back."

Commissioning Scott to vent his opinions was like milking a rattlesnake; once you got his fangs in the jar, the venom just kept coming, and you were sure to have a saleable, if highly toxic, commodity. "A Canadian Bestiary" did cause a small stir. But Scott quickly returned to Essaouira, and I read nothing further by him until his *Helmet of Flesh* finally hit the shelves in 1986.

The first half of the novel is a mildly satirical, third-person narrative about a youngish Canadian—another Symons clone called York Mackenzie - who falls in with a dissolute group of travelling English expatriates in Morocco. In a vigorous extended passage at the centre of the novel, an ecstatic fire dance—"James sniffing the flames like wine...Flesh fused to flame in a single groaning dance"—culminates in what may or may not be a human sacrifice. A fever-ridden Mackenzie then recovers from his hallucinations in a private sanatorium. It becomes evident that York Mackenzie, like Hugh Anderson before him, is in a psychologically precarious state. Unfortunately, from then on, the story rather falls apart as the author doesn't seem to know how to utilize the impact of his vivid central scene. One chapter, a flash-back to his life with a lover called John in Newfoundland, is written mostly in Newfie dialect, which soon becomes annoying. At one point in the book, Mackenzie recalls being beaten up in a Yorkville alley on orders from John's relatives—an event which the real John did not remember from their time together, remarking that back-alley beatings had never been his family's style. Eventually, Mackenzie returns to Newfoundland, and to John, without much apparent enthusiasm.

Helmet of Flesh met with a varied reception. A careful blurb from Margaret Atwood described it as "significant and provocative...will be read and talked about for many years to come." So discerning a connoisseur of humour as Dr. Northrop Frye professed to find it "funny." Others were disappointed, judging it an unsuccessful amalgam of its editor's jovial *Boys' Own* adventure story approach and Scott's inchoate ravings. Some *Helmet* readers were surprised to see Scott's gracious acknowledgement of ongoing assistance from the Canada Council, the Toronto and Ontario Arts Councils, and an array of patrons, named and unnamed, including "businessmen and women, writers, media people, restauranteurs, civil servants and a Toronto bank" - an apparent contradiction of his frequent contention that he had been generally anathematized, blackballed, driven into exile.

Over the years, curious bits of Scott Symons lore filtered back to Canada. The would-be gay messiah was now said to disdain gays, the gay movement, and even Trudeau's legalization of homosexuality. Symons claimed now to "hate Trudeau with a volcanic passion." His sexual preferences, he maintained, in a conversation with David Warren of the *Ottawa Citizen*, had been "a mistake" and "a red herring." What he really wanted, he said, was a "male revolution" against the "epistemological enormities" of feminism, the cruel Canadian women, with their "closed cunts."

In 1990, a Toronto magazine, *The Idler,* published two of Scott's essays. "Atwood-as-Icon" was a critique of the public reputation of Margaret Atwood. It made some telling observations, but was hampered by its author's appearing to have read only one or two of Atwood's works. "Mazo Was Murdered" was not so much a defence of the prolific, now underrated novelist Mazo de la Roche, as an attack on the detractors of her epic *Jalna* series and the Anglo-Canadian cultural tradition it represents. Both essays were included in Christopher Elson's compendium *Dear Reader: Selected Scott Symons*, which Gutter Press published in 1998. Shortly before the book appeared, Canadian filmmaker Nik Sheehan was putting the finishing touches on his documentary film about Scott. *God's Fool* will stand with Charles Taylor's essay as an authoritative documentation of Scott's unique personality.

One old friend interviewed in the film remembers Scott and his wife attending an art gallery function, Scott playing the part of a snake charmer, with his wife as the snake. A former student remarks, "It was very important for him to believe that he loved women." His protégé Donald Martin sees him as essentially a truth-teller, and an influential social force, while

David Gilmour recalls the darker aspects of Scott's self-promotion, and remembers his own incredulous youthful reaction to the massive, uncut *Helmet of Flesh:* "Where is the valium? Oh, this *is* the Valium!"
    Scott himself declares that he is a spiritual African: "I love Morocco
and the Moroccans love me...*Je suis Zulu!*" he adds with a chuckle. And he
supplies an entirely fictional version of his long-ago meeting with John
McConnell.

The school hallway in Muskoka has now become a forest
through which John rides with the wind in his hair, a romantic young Tar-
tar on a galloping horse, confronting Scott in a scene reminiscent of Marlon
Brando eyeing Robert Forster in John Huston's 1967 homo-gothic *Reflec-
tions in a Golden Eye*. In Scott's recapitulation, John teasingly calls him a
big, black bear—not a tame bear like Ms. Engel's mangy mascot, but a wild
animal with impressive, horse-frightening power.

    The Scott Symons that Nik Sheehan captures in his Moroccan re-
doubt appears to have lost much of his vitality, delivering many of his
speeches while lying down. By the end of the film he seems bloated, desperate, and somehow unclean, his watchful eyes shifty and menacing as he
wanders through his lonely compound ranting "How *dare* they!" to the
walls, or making notebook entries in a deserted rooftop restaurant. One
can't help thinking of Big Daddy's resonant line in *Cat on a Hot Tin Roof:*
"There's an air of *mendacity* in this house!" Scott's companion of almost
twenty years, Aaron Klokeid, is seen briefly, but never speaks.

    Regrettably absent from the large cast of commentators in *God's
Fool* is Charles Taylor, whose finances kept Scott in pocket and out of trouble for almost thirty years. In fact Taylor had been very ill, and died before
the film was made. It was the unexpected demise of his true friend and patron at the age of 63 that brought down a slow curtain on Scott's Moroccan
sojourn. Early in 2000, Nik Sheehan, now back in Canada, received two
long-distance calls from Morocco. The first was from the Canadian embassy
in Rabat, informing him that Scott had been instructed to leave the country
within twenty-four hours. The second was from an emotionally shattered
Aaron Klokeid, now apparently "abandoned to his fate."

    Within a week, Scott was back in Toronto, with a colourful story to
explain his sudden reversal of fortune. The mild-mannered Aaron, he confided to Nik Sheehan and others, had become "mixed up in a Thugee ritual
murder cult involving international drug smugglers." Scott's personal investigations into this sinister conspiracy had so rattled the Moroccan authorities that, Scott's connections to the King notwithstanding, he had seen
fit to leave, turning over his "ranch" to the local villagers as a parting gift.

    The word from Morocco was somewhat different. There it was main-
tained that Scott had used Charles Taylor's final subsidy to have an additional turret added to the writing room of his large house. With the loss of
his sole source of income, Scott's many substantial debts to local businesses soon came due, and the government, anxious to avoid further unpleasantness, had issued an expulsion order. Aaron Klokeid, left to his own
devices, was apparently bailed out by his Vancouver family.

By the time Scott arrived back in his birthplace, many of the principal players from the old days had quit the scene. After many years abroad,
Edward Lacey had succumbed to a heart attack in a Toronto rooming house
in 1995. Michael Higgins had returned to England. Richard Phelan and
Michael Pearl had both died in the pandemic that devastated the North
American gay community in the 80s and 90s. By the onset of the Millen-
nium, so many of my old friends had been lost to AIDS that I was not surprised to hear that John McConnell too was now said to be "very sick."

Scott had arrived in Toronto with no money and in deteriorating
health. He first sought shelter at Massey College where his old chum John
Fraser was now Master, but, alas, they were "full up." After a brief stay
next door at Trinity, he prevailed on a succession of friends including Nik
Sheehan and crime writer James Dubro. For a while he lived unobtrusively
in the basement of a fraternity house before being ejected by the authorities. From there he decamped to what Dubro described as "flea-bag rooming
houses" in Kensington Market. I caught up to him in 2001 at a literary get-
together memorializing Edward Lacey. He seemed much mellowed and had
apparently pardoned me for my act of *lèse-majesté* all those years before.

Scott spent his last years living at Leisure World, a crowded care
home for the indigent infirm on St. George Street near the U. of T. Campus.
In 2006 he shared dinner at my home in Toronto's east end, and gave what
was to be his last interview. After several heart attacks and the onset of
Parkinson's and diabetes, he was frail, a bit forgetful, and still eager to
talk. Though much of the old bombast was gone, there were some new delu-
sions (he believed the Prime Minister was his nephew). But he seemed a
different creature from the desperate wreck captured at the end of *God's
Fool.* Nicer, and more tranquil.

His reminisced about his old publisher Jack McClelland, who, he
said, had considered Scott "the most important writer in his stable," but "I
was kind of a peripatetic scandal and he wanted to protect himself." I asked
him about his relationship with John. He had fond memories of their time
in Newfoundland, and was proud that he had been asked to "give the
Christmas address at the Salvation Army Church." His split with John, like
his earlier split with his wife, he blamed wholly on parental malice: "They
threatened to disinherit John and jail me," he said, and had hired a psychiatrist to convince John "there was nothing significant in our relationship."
John's mother, he emphasized, "was a cruel woman." John, he told me, had
wanted to get back together with Scott but had contracted AIDS and "died a
horrible death." Aaron Klokeid, he said, had been in Morocco on his honey-
moon when they met. At that encounter, Scott had apparently played the
role of Julien Green but in this case, the impressionable young man did not
turn away from the older expatriate writer and take his bride back to Canada but stayed with him for two decades. Eventually, he said, Aaron was
"seduced by the governor's mistress."

He much enjoyed his dinner with us, was gracious to my elderly
mother, and posed for a few photos in the garden. Scott seemed in his last

phase to shuck off many of the psychic burdens that had made him so angry. In spite of Leisure World's painfully crowded conditions, he was cared for reasonably well there and had no problem fitting in with the other patients, who called him "the professor" (at least those who could speak). He continued to enjoy his cigarettes, and had at least one outing a week, attending regular Sunday services at St. Thomas's Anglican Church nearby. All in all, he seemed if not content, at least resigned. I never heard him complain. Perhaps all those stays in the monastery rubbed off on the old Monster after all.

Not everything was sweetness and light of course. A publisher friend took him out one evening to dinner and drinks at a Bloor Street restaurant. When Pierre Trudeau's name came up in conversation, Scott grew agitated, stopping all conversation in the room and turning diners' heads by shouting "I fucked that Trudeau up the ass!"—an historic claim that, had it been true, we would surely have heard about before.

Shortly after our interview, I ran into an old Toronto friend of John's, Ian Turner, who told me Scott had been misinformed: John McConnell was in fact alive and well, and living in San Diego! I was able to contact him by email and a few days later, paid a visit to Leisure World to give Scott the good news of his ex-lover's resurrection.

John phoned Scott on Christmas Eve, 2006. Scott apparently expressed no regrets. (Regrets had never been his style.) The brief call, John told me, brought back "all his hyperbole, his exaggerated self-importance and his embellishment of fact to make himself look grand." Yet their talk reminded him "how badly I had needed that kind of dominating, patriarchal presence when I was younger, and how little I felt 'owned' by my own father in an emotional sense." He remained grateful for all the affection that Scott had given him which with time outweighed the acrimony, the abuse, the stolen photographs, and the black eye.

Scott and John spoke several more times, Scott still unapologetic, still urging John to return because "we owe it to ourselves." He remained estranged from his wife and son, and the rest of his family seldom visited, though he did have at least one dinner with his brother Tom. Scott said his brother admitted: "You were right." He didn't mean about everything of course, but specifically about the recognition of gay people in Canada, the public acknowledgement of our humanity, our mortality.

Scott's Anglican funeral service at St. Thomas's was accompanied by clouds of frankincense and every rite in the book—entirely appropriate, one parishioner remarked, as Scott was convinced he would be with the saints. At the Massey College reception afterwards, old friends and acquaintances reminisced. One woman recalled being in Grade Seven with Scott and going to a party with him and another child. Scott, she said, played the accordion at the time. He painted the other kids' faces and had them jump about all evening, telling them "I'll be the organ-grinder and you can be the monkeys!" I related the old classmate's story to John in San Diego. He replied that "it is as good a metaphor of Scott's life as any. In both his life and his writing he portrayed others by painting a false face on them, and then had them dance to his tune, calling them monkeys, which is how they appeared to him."

What drew me to Scott Symons in the first place? He and I were both idiosyncratic writers going our own way, both speaking and naming the Love that Dare Not, writing about what Scott called "homosentience" in the then-thawing emotional climate of the True North. More than that, both of us fell head-over-heels in love with spectacularly beautiful, quite unusual seventeen-year olds who strolled, or strode, into our arms. But Scott was bound to his native Canada in ways that I, as an immigrant, could not be. Scott could never put Rosedale behind him, or the Pink Lady, or his betrayal of boyhood love. Rather, they remained the centre of a psychic world in which he was "eternally thirteen," eternally being told his cock was dirty.

Rating writers is a futile academic exercise. We have no idea how the future will judge our contemporaries. All we know is that we would almost certainly be surprised. Many of the best-known Canadian authors are, though entirely worthy of respect, nonetheless just a tad on the boring side. Scott, on the other hand, was a literary high roller with an utterly unique voice. His name is high on the alternate list with Émile Nelligan, Emily Carr, Grey Owl, Brion Gysin, Juan Butler, bpnichol, Albert Collignon, bill bissett, Norman Elder, Tomson Highway, Lawrence Ytzhak Braithwaite …What a roster! Self-starters and visionaries all.

Canadians of course, had seen something like Scott's bombastic mythologising before, in the robust figure of Irving Layton. But through all Layton's boasts—including his claim to have been born circumcised, the sure sign of a messiah—we could see, or thought we could see, the twinkle in the poet's eye. Scott was every bit as megalomaniacal as Layton, but those black, beady little eyes did not twinkle. Indeed, they seemed (until near the end) not so much searching as accusatory, inquisitorial, confrontational. As for his chequered career (or rather careers, as he had several), Jack McClelland stated it as simply as anyone: "The problem as we see it is that (Scott's) lack of discipline is killing him both as a man and as a writer." His towering ambition attempted the well-nigh impossible: to be the exalted ruler and the insurgent rebel, the hierophant and the heretic, at the same time—a precarious double act attempted by many, Wilde, Mayakovsky, Capote and Mapplethorpe among them. Most came to grief.

Such artists belong to a class of human beings the French call *les monstres sacrés*—Sacred Monsters. They are compulsively, often prolifically creative creatures, utterly self-absorbed, confident of their own charismatic genius, oblivious to the feelings of others, uncaring or unaware about the effects of their own words or actions. They can be bombastic and demanding. They are often profligate with money, sex, drugs, travel, religion: with them, it is all or nothing. At their most monstrous, they can be paranoid, bullying, "a must to avoid." Picasso, Hemingway, Frederick Rolfe "Baron Corvo," Aleister Crowley and Ayn Rand are remembered as classic Sacred Monsters of their century…Scott Symons was surely of their number, which is why Robert Fulford's *mot juste* drew blood. Of his fellow Monsters, it may be the dreaded Rolfe whom Scott most resembles—in his not quite definable talent, his enormous sense of entitlement, his unerring capacity for self-sabotage.

The English writer Daniel Farson had the dubious privilege of knowing more than a few such Monsters, including Francis Bacon and Brendan Behan, and in his book *Sacred Monsters* (Bloomsbury, 1988) he succinctly summed them all up: "They may be difficult, temperamental, occasionally treacherous, frequently drunk, usually unpredictable; this is their price for making life more interesting for the rest of us. They are worth the trouble."

Scott Symons certainly made peoples' lives more interesting, for better or worse. He was a unique writer. And at a signal time in the country's history, he presented us with a reminder that there are many Canadas, not all of them yet mapped. He was the *féderaste par excellence*. He was no saint. But he may well be with them—in one capacity or another.

A Hiss in the Honeysuckle:
Robin Hardy, Earle Birney, Mrs. Claire Oddie and Me

The lonely sunsets flare forlorn
Down valleys dreadly desolate;
The lordly mountains soar in scorn,
As still as death, as stern as fate.

- Robert W. Service, *Songs of a Sourdough*

In the summer of 1980 I was living in a shared house in Finsbury Park, a run-down area of London, with Jamie Perry, a teenaged wizard I had met on the streets of New York two years earlier. Russell, our landlord, brought us a letter from my friend Robin Hardy, who had been working and travelling, organizing gay groups in Thunder Bay and Sudbury and around Ontario. I had told Robin of the trip to Stonehenge Jamie and I had planned. "How I want to walk into that stone circle," he wrote, "and lay my hands upon the monoliths and watch the moon rise....I have for years had a fantasy in which I press my body against one of the upright stones and rub my crotch to orgasm...."

Robin had been a close friend of mine and would later be part of the magickal order Jamie founded when we moved our home base to Canada. I had last heard from him in November of 1979 when we were both in Toronto. He sent a letter apologising for missing a date; he had been working hard and feeling strangely "empty," he said. "Quite literally exhausting" himself, he had come down with the flu. "I feel inarticulate," he had written, "and my body aches." Now he was looking forward to travelling to Europe, and we were hoping to meet up soon. I worried about him.

I first met Robin Hardy at the University of Toronto during a packed, lively debate between the American novelist John Rechy and the Canadian sociologist John Alan Lee. The subject was S/M. Rechy was emotional, irrational and charming, making Lee, the more logical thinker, appear cold by comparison. As the debate played out, my ears kept listening but my eyes wandered. I noticed the tall, handsome young man standing across the room from me, and when he asked a perceptive question of the debaters - about the imagery in commercial gay porn — I added a brief remark of my own. After the talk, we sought each other out. Robin had a puckish quality I found irresistible. We went to bed together, and began a friendship that lasted into the 1990s.

Robin and I were both part of the Stonewall generation, young homosexual men involved in the Canadian Gay Liberation movement during the 1970s. I was a university dropout; Robin had graduated from the prestigious Dalhousie Law School, but threw over a legal career to become an unpaid activist for the gay cause, then still impeded and obscured by legal shadows. His journalism paid for — and was part of — his activism. As a writer, he was by nature a free lance, and a free spirit; neither academic prose nor conventional journalism appealed to him. As both of us had left academia to write, and to work in the gay movement, our paths inevitably converged at *The Body Politic* whose offices on Duncan Street were a few yards from Robin's apartment. Robin and I both wrote for *The BP*. I handed in my small press book review column every month and wrote an occasional article; Robin was closer to the Inner Circle (it always amused him when I called it the Body Politbureau). Later he became the Canadian movement's first full-time, paid political operative, a roving organizer for the Coalition for Gay Rights in Ontario. He was an eloquent reporter who brought a fresh approach and a quicksilver sensibility to his subjects.

Robin and I would only occasionally talk about writing (or, rather, about trying to get published, difficulties with editors and problems with bouncing cheques). Our connection was friendly, erotic, not particularly literary. Robin was good-humoured, brilliant, masculine, gentle, and utterly unaffected. He had a turned-up nose, Cupid's lips, the body of the young Johnny Weissmuller and the eyes of an elf. Moving in different circles, he and I would get together from time to time, usually in Toronto or New York. I remember one Greenwich Village excursion we made in order to spend some of Robin's newly awarded grant money on a particular pair of cowboy boots—a hint, maybe, of his ultimate destination in the American South-West.

Some time in the early Eighties, we took a trip together to the Rhode Island countryside to visit my friend Joe Kadlec. Joe lived in a rented clapboard house on a winding, picturesque road in the woods—the property of a nearby nuclear plant. The white-painted cabin was sparsely furnished, like all Joe's accommodations, but he had prepared a big double bed in the spare room for me and Robin. I have a little group of black & white photos showing the three of us and Joe's friend Julie—her father supervised the plant - wandering among the field of honeysuckle that grew by a little pond near the house, Robin and I feeding each other honeysuckle flowers, drinking the nectar from their small, yellow blossoms.

One morning with Joe and Julie back at the house for lunch, Robin and I headed toward a little hill a mile away. In the pocket of the jacket I was wearing I had a beat-up ex-library copy of Earle Birney's *The Strait of Anian*, published in 1948 and found in a dollar dump bin on one of my routine hunts. From the Fifties through the Eighties, Earle Birney, author of the humorous war novel *Turvey*, was recognized as one of Canada's leading poets. According to his biographer Elspeth Cameron, the young Birney had taken a strong interest in the work of the homosexual emancipationist Edward Carpenter, a disciple of Walt Whitman. He had written an early story, "Night," about cruising, and during his university years had been a protégé of the gay English professor G.G. "Doc" Sedgwick. The mature Birney was best known for his narrative poem "David," about a pair of young men on a tragic mountain climbing expedition. Mourning his dead friend, Birney's narrator remarks, in the poem's closing lines, that "none but the sun and incurious clouds have lingered / Around the marks of that day... That day, the last of my youth, on the last of our mountains." The poem was so vividly moving that many readers believed it had actually happened, leading Al Purdy to start referring to Birney as "the man who killed David." I first encountered "David" in high school—chillingly declaimed by a favourite

TOP LEFT: "Esprit de bois/Uncut", self-portrait of Robin Hardy. Photograph courtesy of the New York Public Library.

Top Right: River of Flesh *by "Jack Hild" (Robin Hardy). (Harlequin Books, 1985), front cover.*

BOTTOM: Robin Hardy (centre) with Joe Kadlec (left) and Ian Young, among the honeysuckle.

teacher, one day when we were supposed to be practicing French verbs.

Another poem in the same book was a long elegy called "For Steve," about a friend killed in action in World War II. A moving poem, it was omitted from Birney's *Selected Poems*, and when, a few years later, the same publisher issued a two-volume *Collected Poems,* "For Steve," which could not reasonably be left out, appeared with a small, one word alteration. The lines "It's not alone because you too were gay / and are gone, Steve, that the swing of your arms haunts me today" had been slightly but significantly altered. In the revised version, the word "gay" had been changed to read "game," and I amused Robin by saying that "You too were game" made me think of the old movie "The Naked Prey" where a more-or-less denuded Cornel Wilde staggers through the jungle, hunted by relentless savages. When the poem was written, in the late 1940's, only those in the know would have recognized "gay" as a code word for homosexual. But by 1975 when the slipcased, two-decker *Collected Poems* was solemnly deposited in the National Library, what had once been underground argot had become a widely recognized term, and Birney had acquired a public reputation as a lusty heterosexual. The change went virtually unnoticed, but there, hidden in plain sight, was one of the keys to Dr. Birney's closet. But the poem Robin and I took turns reading that day, stretching out on the hillock, smoking a joint, was the perennial favourite, "David," the classic Canadian tragedy about youth, love, guilt, and death.

Pleasantly high, we wandered off to visit a certain deep pool hidden in the nearby woods, which, so it was said, was home to a brood of giant, parthenogenetic snapping turtles. As if on cue, the two largest of these, known as Rita and Mama, swam readily to the surface to gobble up the food scraps we threw to them. They had ferocious-looking talons on their front limbs and faces reminiscent of mediaeval gargoyles. The claim of parthenogenesis may well have originated with one of the local residents, "old Howard," who swore that in his many years of catching, "sexing" and releasing them, he had never found a male, only females. I couldn't help wondering, a) why did he bother?; b) what difficulties might bedevil such an enterprise; and c) was old Howard just having everyone on? But my brief visit with Robin allowed no time to explore these local mysteries.

Our friendship was complicated by an episode that occurred at the beginning of the 1980s involving an accomplished con artist whom I'll call Mrs. Claire Oddie. I had met, and become lovers with, the seventeen-year old magician Jamie Perry in New York City in 1978. He moved to Toronto late in 1980 and, as he had in New York, soon collected around him a small group of people interested in ceremonial magick. Robin became one of the first members of our group where he was known as Brother Goodfellow, a name Jamie gave him, harking back to the half human, half fairy trickster of English legend. The name Robin had once been associated with Merlin, with the penis and with the horned god of the witches. And as it happened, our Robin possessed, just south of his ribcage, a supernumery nipple such as witches were thought to have. Later, he would fall in with Harry Hay's

Radical Faeries where he initiated the "faeries' hiss" which became popular at their gatherings as a sort of sibilant group approval.

Jamie often bought incense from a local occult shop where an effusive woman who greeted everyone with a brutal bear-hug quickly offered to rent him a room in her two-storey flat. I disliked Mrs. Claire Oddie on sight but as Jamie accepted her as a friend and was in immediate need of temporary lodgings, I fell in with their arrangements. Mrs. Oddie rented the top two floors of an old, three-storeyed duplex in the west end of the city, subletting the two extra bedrooms—one to a quiet young couple, the other to Jamie. She told us that the female lover who had shared the rooms with her had absconded with the rent money, which now had to be made up.

Claire Oddie had become something of a cause célèbre in the gay and lesbian community. She was apparently a refugee from the U.S. and was fighting a protracted, international legal battle with her ex-husband for custody of their two young children. Though the children were living with her, legal custody had been denied, supposedly because Mrs. Oddie had been living openly as a lesbian. A fund had been set up to pay for her legal expenses and Queer activists harangued many crowds on her behalf. She seemed to have no lack of money and took taxis everywhere. Loud and burly with Medusa locks and a riveting stare, she was full of stories about her abusive, born-again ex-husband, and her harrowing history as a multiple rape victim. She hurled herself into everyone's affairs with intense gusto and many unfunny jokes.

After Jamie and I had handed over a couple of months rent, things began falling apart in the rented duplex. Mrs. Oddie went missing for days at a time, stealing in and out late at night. The waterbed in her locked room emptied its contents onto the floor, warping the polished hardwood and damaging the ceiling in the room downstairs. Mrs. Oddie became aggressively belligerent about small things: there was no string; we had left the kitchen light on...Also, she confided, the Indian couple who occupied the third bedroom were not paying their way. Dashing out on one of her mysterious trips, she warned us that the landlady who owned the building might come by. We were under no circumstances to talk to her; she was an unpleasant Ukrainian whose sinister background had something to do with the War.

When the landlady eventually materialized, she left a note under the door and I made arrangements to meet her at her home, a large, pleasant house on a tree-lined, upper middle-class street in the city's West end. Mrs. Sawchuk, who seemed not only too nice but too young to have been a Nazi war criminal, served me tea and cakes as we compared notes.

According to Mrs. Sawchuk, Claire Oddie's room-mate had been the original tenant of the suite and had fled after Mrs. Oddie pocketed the rent and screamed at her once too often. None of the money Jamie or the young couple paid had ever reached Mrs. Sawchuk. I forked over a cheque (which left a gaping hole in my bank account) and we parted on good terms; Jamie and I would take over the lease or find a new place as soon as we could.

Before any new arrangements could be made, Claire Oddie reappeared, bearing new locks for all the doors and accompanied by one of the more dubious denizens of the witchy shop, a bearded ex-convict biker called Raunchy, who proceeded to threaten us with physical violence if we didn't get out immediately, leaving our possessions behind as payment for "money owed." At that point, I thought of going to the police. But Jamie's papers were not exactly in order and wouldn't be for some time; we preferred not to draw attention to his temporary lack of a Landed Immigrant certificate. Then Jamie remembered that he had left his bedroom window open just a crack. With the help of a tall ladder borrowed from a garden shed, Jamie crawled in the third floor window and unlocked his door from the inside. We piled everything into two taxicabs and took off into the night.

Mrs. Oddie quickly got word to us that she had laid charges of assault and theft against us both. We had, she reminded us, thrown her down a flight of stairs and stolen her property; arrest warrants had been issued and the cops were after us. In addition, she warned, Raunchy was so indignant at our vile treatment of her that he had vowed to kill us, and she was powerless—*powerless*—to prevent it. Surrounded by this nonsense and chaos, Jamie desperately needed another temporary place to stay. Robin stepped into the breach. Though his apartment was small, he invited Jamie to stay there until we sorted things out. At Robin's place, surrounded by boxes of Jamie's belongings, I phoned the police to ask whether there were any outstanding warrants for either Jamie or myself. There weren't.

It was from Robin that I began to learn more about Mrs. Claire Oddie's curious background. She had become a public figure, at least among gays and lesbians, through her fight to regain legal custody of her young son and daughter. Her story was that custody had been awarded to her abusive, born-again Christian husband on the grounds that Mrs. Oddie had begun living with a female lover. On this basis, she was able to rally the gay and lesbian community behind her through a series of incendiary press releases and fund-raising events. I attended one rally in which the lesbian activist Chris Bearchell, a stocky young woman who needed no public address system, hectored the crowd while buckets passed among them, filling with money.

Before her arrival on the gay scene, Robin told me, Mrs. Oddie had cut a swath through the Trotskyist and independent Marxist groups in various Canadian cities, using her claims of persecution as a union activist to pay for her taxi-taking lifestyle and leaving many angry International Socialists in her considerable wake. Dark stories circulated that she had framed a mildly retarded gay man for rape and sent him to prison.

By the time the second phase of her child custody case came to trial, Mrs. Oddie was claiming loudly that her former husband had sexually abused the children. Her female attorney, a well-known local feminist, called the little boy to the witness stand to confirm these allegations, entering the child's neatly-written diary in evidence. Upon cross-examination, it turned out that although the boy had indeed written in his diary about being abused by Daddy, it was Mommy who had told him what to write; no abuse had ever occurred. Mommy's case collapsed and Daddy was awarded custody. Mrs. Oddie's response was to kidnap the kids and lead the authorities on a zig-zag cross-country chase until she was finally hunted down a few thousand miles west of town.

Having exhausted gays, lesbians and Marxists as sources of funds and sympathy, Mrs. Oddie later popped up again in the Wiccan community, claiming to be not only a lesbian but a witch too, *and* a cancer survivor. No-one questioned her claims until Jamie alerted people to the public record. After a brief hiatus, she resurfaced yet again, this time as the Indian maiden "Brenda Two Feathers," a courageous "two-spirited woman with HIV," reaping diverse benefits from sympathetic care-givers and the burgeoning AIDS industry. The pathetic story of her diagnosis and subsequent struggle with despair moved many to tears and Mrs. Oddie was able to expand her continuing career as a professional victim.

Robin, as it happened, knew about Mrs. Oddie's checkered past through his friend Chris Bearchell, an ally in *The Body Politic's* ongoing factional infighting. I was grateful to Robin for helping us out, but puzzled as to why he hadn't warned me, or even dropped a hint, about Mrs. Oddie when she first asked us for money. At any rate, Jamie and I found new lodgings, Mrs. Oddie continued her legal battles (without her attorney who understandably jumped ship along the way) and the whole business soon blew over.

No real harm had been done, but I couldn't help wondering why Robin had kept silent. When he saw us about to step over the cliff, why didn't he tap us on the shoulder and say, "Hey guys, there's something you should know..."? Had Chris sworn him to silence? Had he simply been caught up in political correctness, ideology overriding any other considerations? This was an aspect of Robin I hadn't seen before and didn't really understand - a passivity in time of crisis, an apparent propensity to stand back and let things proceed toward a possible disaster.

Shortly after Robin wrote an eerily prophetic short story called "The Day the Homos Disappeared," the first early reports of AIDS began to be noticed. Jamie, in spite of having numerous instances of "unsafe sex" with various men who turned out to be HIV Positive, persisted in testing Negative, i.e. apparently uninfected. Then in 1988, after a catastrophic illness precipitated by a work injury, he tested Positive for the first time. After a trip to the Middle East in 1993 he was misdiagnosed with amoebic parasites, hospitalized, and given a strong drug, Septra, to which he was known to be allergic. To alleviate a violent and alarming reaction, he was given a second drug - at double the required dose. The hospital sent him home, where he died, surrounded by friends, on World AIDS Day, December 1, 1993.

Though we stayed in touch, I saw little of Robin in Jamie's last years. He had travelled around Canada and spent time in New York and

Berlin before moving to Tucson, Arizona. In the last phone call he made to me, he asked whether I would be interested in helping ghost-write some of the men's adventure stories he, John Preston and others were working on—military tales with the homosocial atmosphere common to the genre. I asked him to send copies of some of the books. I can't remember that they ever arrived. In a letter to me, he wrote: "When you're not here, I think of you often, think of things I want to say to you but never do. Somehow is it safe to say you frighten me in ways I'm not sure of. Or perhaps only too sure of. You seem so constant in your affection towards me. While I continue to run to the faceless arms of anonymous strangers, never any more certain of what I'm running from as I am uncertain what I'm running towards. Some kind of defensiveness in solitude. And there you are, unwavering."

If Robin felt inhibited, I felt frustrated. By the 1990s, we had drifted apart. He had tested HIV Positive around the time Jamie did, and the conventional wisdom was that "testing positive" was a kind of death sentence, like seeing a noose in the tea-leaves. Robin wrote that "the words *doomed* or *fatal* appeared in virtually every news report. Repeated often enough, this conjecture became accepted truth, although scientific data have always contradicted it. AIDS is a killer disease. It has not ever been under control. But as scientists are just now getting around to emphasizing, all sorts of people survive HIV infection asymptomatically for decades; others resist infection totally or never become virulent. The evidence for these phenomena has been whispered about for years among people with HIV, but it contradicted the prevalent view that AIDS had to mean death. For more than a decade, the most pervasive opportunistic infection of AIDS, and one engendered by the power of the medical establishment, was despair."

Robin never despaired enough, or hoped enough, to take AZT, a highly toxic rejected cancer drug that was then being redirected to AIDS patients. He said the sulfa drugs he took for his minor skin problems gave him meningitis. Yet in spite of his caution about medications and his realization that "we're written off as soon as we walk in the door," he wrote, in what would become the opening passage of his posthumous book, that "HIV ticks like a silent time bomb in my veins. My blood and semen are poison to my species. My body has been commandeered by a lethal alien..."

It was during this period that Robin wrote the only novel to appear over his own name, *Call of the Wendigo*. This is a story about a group of Canadian teenagers who encounter a supernatural killer. A shape-shifting monster with a heart of ice, it infiltrates people's thoughts, steals their free will, makes friends try to kill each other, feeds on human flesh, and leaves a distinctive track. Its name is Wendigo, a creature from native mythology, but it is not difficult to see it as a stand-in for another mythical monster, HIV, the demonic retrovirus whose name is always written in capital letters.

While in Berlin in the late 1980s, Robin became involved with a sinister skinhead-cum-businessman who liked to play murderous games and enjoyed threatening Robin's life. "That little dance with death," David Groff wrote, "made the coitus even sweeter, especially in retrospect." Robin believed that it was this man, whom he calls Rollo, who had infected him. In his last, unfinished, book he describes a time when Rollo almost strangled him while they were having sex. Afterwards Robin fell ill with what seemed to be a bad case of the flu. Later, diagnosed HIV Positive, he came to believe it was that particular sexual act that caused his seroconversion. And he began to regard himself as a kind of murder victim, with Rollo as the murderer—a fascinating monster with a heart of ice, who feeds on human flesh.

By the mid-Nineties, Robin had written several insightful articles for the *Village Voice* which he began developing into a book about gay men, brotherhood and sexual desire in the age of AIDS, to be called *The Landscape of Death*.[2] And he had moved to Arizona, where, according to a friend, he lived an "almost monastic" life. In October, 1995, he sent the half-finished manuscript to his agent and set out with his friend Ted on a mountain-climbing expedition in the Tonto National Forest, east of Phoenix.

Away from their campsite one evening, Robin and Ted were hurrying to make it back before dark set in. Taking a shortcut down a ravine, Robin slipped and fell, breaking his leg badly. Ted picked his way down the cliff to be with Robin; if he left to get help he couldn't be sure of finding his way back in the gathering darkness. According to David Groff's account. the two friends spent the night braced against the side of the ravine. Ted built a fire and they talked, though Robin, his shattered left leg "tangled beneath him," slipped in and out of delerium. Robin remarked that he had forgotten to make a propitiation to Hermes before setting out.

David Groff writes that "when dawn finally came, Ted positioned Robin as comfortably as he could and scrambled upward onto the plane of the desert. He turned and took a photograph of Robin before he rushed off to seek help." But by the time he returned, Robin had fallen into the ravine and died.

A phone call from a friend woke me early one morning in the autumn of 1995 to tell me of Robin's death at the age of 43. I thought over the good times we'd shared, and particularly our holiday in the Rhode Island countryside, when we sat together reading Earle Birney's poetry. Bob, the narrator of Birney's poem "David," tells of his friend falling off a ledge while they are mountain climbing, and landing with his legs splayed beneath him. Badly hurt and paralysed, David asks Bob to help him die by easing him over the side of the cliff. Bob makes his way back to the camp: "I said that he fell straight to the ice where they found him, / And none but the sun and incurious clouds have lingered / Around the marks of that day on the ledge of the Finger, / That day, the last of my youth, on the last of our mountains."

---

2. Robin's manuscript was completed by his editor David Groff and published in 1999 as *The Crisis of Desire: AIDS and the Fate of Gay Brotherhood*.

48 ENCOUNTERS WITH AUTHORS

David did not want to survive in a paralysed body. Robin, committed to his half-finished book, had a reason to hang on. Yet how could I not feel his death as an eerie recapitulation of David's in the poem we both knew so well? David Groff wrote that "Robin Hardy may have fallen to his death, but he also died of AIDS." Groff meant that it was AIDS that had taken him to that spot, and that AIDS "made him hurry." But I wondered: in those last hours, cold, half delirious and in pain, could Robin's belief that if he survived, it might only be to die of a terrible illness, have made the difference between hanging on and falling?

What is the Wendigo anyway? What does its call sound like? Why was Robin so fascinated by its monstrous myth? Robin was only one of many young men I've known who "died of AIDS" while actually dying of something else entirely. My friend John Wadey was diagnosed HIV Positive and told he had a year and half to live. His attempts to drown his sorrow in drink and drugs didn't work; his strong constitution kept him healthy. Eventually his over-indulgence caused his promising business to fail. In despair, he contemplated suing the hospital that had pronounced his death sentence. When neither HIV nor addiction could kill him, he took an Exacto-knife to his throat—and survived even that. Eventually, he retreated to a basement apartment in his adoptive parents' home, where, according to his obituary, he "passed away peacefully."

Many HIV-Positives—like Jamie—have died from the side-effects of their prescription drugs. Others, like another fellow *Body Politic* contributor Danny Cockerline, committed suicide. Yet HIV alone has never been proven to cause AIDS, and there is even scientific debate about its existence as a discrete entity. Could it be a mere marker for immune suppression—a conjectural phantom, like the Wendigo? Whatever the truth about AIDS, belief that one has contracted it often has fatal consequences.

Robin's two brothers, Charles and Christopher, both suffered from cystic fibrosis, an inherited, often fatal glandular disease. Robin helped nurse Christopher before he died at the age of 34. I can't help wondering whether, after his brother's death, Robin might not have suffered from a form of survivor guilt. The large part played by survivor guilt in the AIDS epidemic has been documented by the therapist Walt Odets in his book *In the Shadow of the Epidemic*.

But these are fugitive thoughts, perhaps farfetched, and leading nowhere. Maybe Robin's death on that cold mountain had nothing to do with the loss of his brother, or with his fascination with homicidal lovers, or with Earle Birney's poem—still less with his odd reluctance to warn a friend of possible danger! Nevertheless I couldn't help mulling over questions I couldn't answer—and could barely articulate. "Who killed Cock Robin?"

I had been thinking about Robin Goodfellow on the evening in 2001 when I was to take part in a memorial reading commemorating the Canadian poet Edward Lacey, whose book *Later* I had published in the late 70s. As I entered the pub where the reading was to take place, I spotted the writer John Robert Colombo and went over to speak to him. Colombo and I hadn't seen each other for perhaps a decade, and as I approached him, he saw coming towards him across the room not myself but an old friend of the same height and build—Earle Birney, who had died six years before at the age of 91, less than two months before Robin's fatal accident. I asked John to sign for me the only book of his that I had been able to lay hands on that evening—an "anthology of fact and fantastic fiction" about the Wendigo.

My most vivid recollections of Robin seem now like mere glimpses, still fresh, but unhappily brief, fragments of an happy, affectionate friendship that never quite found its focus. I remember one afternoon being teasingly lead to Robin's "favourite park"—which turned out to be an abandoned railroad yard where he liked to have sex. I remember him stripped to the waist, smashing a doorway in his apartment wall with a huge mallet. I remember him telling me proudly how his mother, a nurse, had refused to have him circumcised. I recall my disappointment that he never made it to Stonehenge with us. And I remember a sunny afternoon we spent in Rhode Island—sipping honeysuckle from the roadside blossoms, content in each other's company, enjoying the day, and blissfully unaware of dark times ahead, as all young men are.

Mrs. Claire Oddie, as it happens, continues on her lucrative odyssey through the many varieties of public victimhood. I saw her picture—under yet another assumed name—on the front page of the Family section of the newspaper a month or so ago. I've forgotten which unfortunate group she was acting as spokesperson for, but the article was extremely sympathetic to her heart-rending plight. Shopping in downtown Toronto a few days later I saw her, laden with shopping bags, sashaying her ample behind up Yonge Street. Hanging around her neck was a large wooden cross. Just as I recognized her, she hailed a cab, heaved her bulk into the back seat, and disappeared into the traffic.

The Trials of Norman Elder

"It's surprising what a friendly place it is - the whole world!"
- Norman Elder

One of the first things a visitor tended to notice on entering the massive, three-storey brick house on Bedford Road was the stuffed emu hanging upside down over the main staircase. After the bright sunlight outside, the sudden gloom might well have obscured the framed collection of Papuan penis gourds immediately opposite the front door, or the array of red and blue prize ribbons plastering the lobby. But even if you missed the gourds and the horse-racing ribbons, the stuffed emu fixed one's attention. As one's eyes adjusted to the low light, more exhibits came into view, crowded among the massive antique furniture: arrangements of shark jaws and monkey bones, stone axes and tribal weapons, a coffin decorated like an ornate wedding cake, display cases filled with mounted Goliath beetles and huge flying insects, a stuffed zebra head surrounded by more equestrian ribbons, an egg from the extinct elephant bird. Above the stairs and partially obscured by the emu hung a striking 8x4 foot painting, a full-length portrait of a young man in a forest of tendrils. From another room, peculiar sounds from resident animals contributed to the unique atmosphere.

For thirty-five years, 140 Bedford Road in Toronto's historic Annex district was the home of explorer, equestrian, painter, writer and local personality Norman Elder, and the location of the Norman Elder Museum and Gallery, repository of curious artefacts from some of the most inaccessible regions of the globe. The gutting of the unique Museum in 2004 and the dispersal and partial destruction of its contents constituted the final chapter of an unusual and ultimately tragic story.

I first met Norman Elder in the summer of 1967, the legendary Summer of Love. In late Sixties Toronto, Rochdale College was briefly thriving as an alternative university, the club scene was jumping, and the Yorkville district had become a favourite destination for hippies and travellers from across the country. A jazz and blues enthusiast in those days, I had visited most of the city's music clubs to hear Sleepy John Estes, Rev. Gary Davis and Woody Herman's Third Herd. I had read my poems at the Bohemian Embassy and the Inn of the Unmuzzled Ox. And I wrote for Ron Thody's irreverent pulp tabloid, *Satyrday.*

I was sitting with Ron in a sidewalk café in Yorkville when Norman Elder stopped to say hello. Norman was then in his late twenties, with a handsome, open countenance that retained its boyish aspect in spite of the beginnings of male pattern baldness. His private Museum and Gallery was then housed across the street from the café. I encountered him again in 1970 when visiting Scott Symons who was lodging with Norm at the same Yorkville location. I remember that along with Norm, Scott, and a collection of large snakes, the Museum was home to a strikingly attractive young man who appeared to be in his late teens. Someone said he was Norman's boyfriend.

My first visit to Norman's Bedford Road mansion was in 1972, when we exchanged books: my first slim chapbook of poetry for a copy of *Noshitaka,* a handsome production by Coach House Press consisting of poetic notes and sketches from a trip to the headwaters of the Amazon, deep in the interior of Peru, near Machu Picchu. This taxing, mind-bending trip was one of the earliest of Norman's countless excursions to remote parts of the world.

Norman's objective, he wrote, was to live among and study the Machiguengas, a tribe that had migrated to the dense jungles of the Upper Amazon during the Inca conquest, reverting to a pre-stone age existence. There, "geographical isolation has produced a uniquely primitive social organization...a strange religious practice and a stoic but dynamic individualism." The Machiguengas are reputed to be head-hunters, eaters of genitals, executors of girl children. They make meals of parrots and monkey-brains, hunting and killing with arrows the chimp-sized howler monkeys that inhabit the forest. They are subject to uncontrolled epidemics and infections that often result in death. Without words for affection or beauty, they are totally survival-oriented, reflecting "a cultural gap of fifty thousand years." Most had never seen the face of an outsider.

Norman's stopping off point for this unusual adventure was, paradoxically, a club for Lima's moneyed equestrian set, "lush to the point of overpowering decadence," an instructive contrast to the wretched squalor of the jungle towns with their half-naked prostitutes, "sperm-drenched gutters" and fetid smell. By comparison, the jungle was another world, immense, weird and hallucinatory. "About this place," he wrote, "the vast Amazonas stretches its 50,000 miles of navigable water tributaries...it nourishes one quarter of the world's forests...eighty-six percent of all things that grow...it breeds more animate species than the rest of the world...its growing rate excels all other earthly things...the eternal anaconda boa is its king...its fearful carnivorous god."

Penetrating deep into the territory of the Machiguengas, Norman discovered a humid, jungle world hostile to every apparent concept of human life. Parrots were "thick as mosquitos" and thorn-covered vines moved "with the dense tensile life...(an) ever-extending layer of intestinal vegetable pulp...Enormous trunks uproot the undergrowth and heave their phallic erection one against another...like animal tendons knotted...pulsating... dripping from severed limbs..." Cancerous white fungi, silhouettes of tangled vines "producing strange jagged fans in the sky's flesh," lush, black organisms that twisted and knotted in the vivid red light and a cacophony of shrieking cries all added to this surrealistic, visionary world.

Here, fourteen-foot fish, poison frogs and giant crocodiles were common, and small, parasitic water creatures could swim into your genitals to feed on their delicate membranes. Bermiflies and screw-worms lay their eggs in your sweat-drenched clothing, burrowing into flesh and hatching white grubs under the skin, producing large abscessed swellings and infected wounds. "Insects," Norman noted, "are breeding in the small of my back." In this environment, common staples of civilization like shoes and leather jackets soon become fetid and useless. Leaving the hut at night to answer the call of nature, the humid air pierced by violent, overpowering shrieks, it was advisable to carry a club to deter attacks by wild dogs. The book's final chapter breaks off unexpectedly. Norman has managed to befriend one of his guides, a young man called Hector. They exchange presents—some carved totems, anaconda skins and monkey skulls in return for a shirt, flashlight and shoes, "all I have except my cut-off jeans and my shotgun." But later there is a falling out when Hector "becomes irksome." Norman sculpts a sand image of Hector and unaccountably stabs its head with a bamboo pole. He immediately regrets what he has done, remembering that in this strange society, perceived insults sometimes lead to suicide. Instead, the sensitive boy's tentative friendship changes into poisonous glares and an avoidance of contact. Finally, surrounded by a cloud of vampire bats, Norman muses on the power of Hector's soul as it merges with a mysterious "ovalistic symbol into the most perfect sympathy of union of two bodies."

Noshitaka is written in an sketchy, poetic style without capital letters, with only ellipses for punctuation, and illustrated with the author's prepared photographs overdrawn with spiky, tangled vines and spidery tendrils. The book resembles accounts of hallucinatory experiences, drug "trips"—except that this trip is a real journey, to a real place on the earth, as far as possible from the neatly tended surroundings of Bedford Road.

The book was attractive and intriguing, but I found its ambiguous conclusion confusing and unsatisfactory. I couldn't help thinking that something important here was hinted at but unstated: "I shall leave unrecorded the rest of my diary." It seemed to me that for all the grisly masochistic splendours of the arboreal forest, the real story here was the story of Norman and Hector—and it had apparently ended badly.

Next to the equestrian trophies in Norman's front lobby was a large, ornate book stand displaying a copy of either Who's Who In the World or Who's Who in Canada, open at an extensive entry for Elder, Norman. Norman was proud—and amused—that his listing occupied the same page as the Queen Mother's. It was there, in his front hall, scrutinizing Who's Who, that I first began to learn about Norman's background.

Norman Elder was born in Toronto on July 17, 1939, the youngest of five children of a manufacturing family with an address on the exclusive Park Lane Circle. His next door neighbour was Conrad Black with whom he was boyhood friends. Educated at Upper Canada College, where he was a reticent student, reluctant to speak up in class, he became an avid equestrian and skydiver, winning his first competitive medals before his tenth birthday. He was also something of a hell-raiser, burning down a historic barn, breaking both arms in fights and getting jailed for vagrancy. When he broke a leg, he continued his sporting activities wearing a cast.

Four years later, Norman and a friend attempted to cross the Sahara in a Jeep, Norman drawing and filming oasis communities and making extensive notes on the sex customs of desert Arabs. In those days, he was describing himself as "a hippie." His family had varied reactions to his idiosyncrasies. His grandmother encouraged him to travel, telling him "it

will be enlightening for you." His father on the other hand seemed pecu-
liarly indifferent. "The first time I came back from the Amazon," Norman
wrote, "I was dying to tell Dad all the details of the trip, but he kept turning
the TV up louder. Then I thought of a great way to get him to listen. I
phoned up (television personality) Betty Kennedy and went on her talk
show."

At the age of twenty Norman won gold and bronze medals in the
Pan-American Games three-day equestrian event. (He won his silver medal
at a later Games.) As a result, he was made captain of the Canadian equestrian team at the 1968 Mexico City Olympics where he shared a mutual love
of horses with Prince Philip, the Duke of Edinburgh. He became friendly
with the Prince, who remarked to him during a long ceremony, "One thing
you learn quickly as a Royal is to never pass up an opportunity to go to the
lavatory."

Stints at the University of Western Ontario and the Banff School of
Fine Arts preceded Norman's second major trip when he used the money
from sales of *Noshitaka* to strike out for Inuit villages in the far Canadian
North and "hitch-hiked to Greenland," a journey that resulted in his second
book, *Oksitartok*, published in 1966 in an edition uniform with *Noshitaka*
and equipped with a Foreword by his friend the 86 year old Lady Eaton.

Oksitartok ('the uninhibited beautiful minds") was dedicated "to the
great globs of raw humanity;" like the earlier book it consists of on-the-spot
journal entries, unredacted notes in sketchy bursts (complete with occasional misspellings and grammatical solecisms) and broken up into short
lines resembling poetry. In this journal account of living, sleeping and
working with the Eskimos (before that term was discarded), Norman com-
ments on the Northern peoples' elusive character and daily habits, their
attitude to their Skidoos ("this machine can't smell the wind") and their
love of Coca-Cola and country music. He observes with pleasure that
among the varied incursions of the modern world, "a primitive element
shone through."

"I feel the same respect and deep honour toward the Eskimo as I did
for the Machiguenga. They personified a superior being...an uncorrupted
purity and honesty of heart." Several times in the book, he returns to
thoughts of the Amazon forest, and to Hector, and a friendship that was
sabotaged by impulsiveness and misunderstanding. In the back of the book
there is a photo of the author with the dates 1939-1989. Like Glenn Gould,
he predicted he would die at fifty. Unlike Gould, he outlived his prediction.

In 1967, Norman made his first trip to New Guinea, hiking 160 km.
into isolated overgrown volcanic highlands to collect artefacts for the Royal
Ontario Museum. He published his account of the trip in *Cannibalistic Catharsis,* the final volume of his self-published trilogy. The people he stayed
with were men naked except for gourds tied over their penises, wild pig
tusks through their noses and quills piercing their cheeks. His aim, he
wrote, was to "tap the untouched resources of human behaviour" in "this
oddest of circumstances, a choking sanctuary of unhygienic native smells, a

blackened thatched atmosphere sealed in smoke, body odours from birth, urine drenched bamboo wall, rot of food residue on dried mud; my new home, alive with humanity." Norman set out on these journeys systematically prepared. He carried his necessities (including insect repellent, antibiotics, cash, and garbage-bags as wrapping for cameras and notebooks) in two army surplus canvas bags, with additional empty bags for artefacts and insect specimens. Black's Film provided free film for some of the trips and Alex Tilley, proprietor of the Tilley clothing company, supplied free shorts and shirts. Many items were intended as gifts. "Shirts are a big thing," he said. One man he met in New Guinea wrote to say he'd "broken" his shirt, "so I sent him fifty." Other trade items included candy and locally-purchased cigarettes, salt and machetes. His mosquito nets and hammocks he gave away at the end of each trip.

"I'm just off running around in the bush like a little kid," he would say with a grin, making light of the taxing, often horrendous conditions - and the recurring dysentery, intestinal parasites and malaria which, inevitably, had to be dealt with. Betty Kennedy, in her Forward to *Cannibalistic Catharsis*, wrote that "Norman is a man who dares simply to be himself...a free spirit...open to all ideas and all people...he has a natural grace that makes him equally at home with sophisticated cosmopolites or strange-tongued primitives...He savors every minute of life."

The late 60's and early 70's were an especially active time, even for Norman. He made his first film, *Alcoholism's Children*, and painted his best known picture, a large, fantastical image of Pierre Trudeau that later made its way to Ottawa; it was said to have adorned Trudeau's outer office for a while. As a graduate architect, he worked for a time as a draftsman for Parkins Associates and joined the Board of Directors of the Ontario Epilepsy Foundation. Supported by the wealthy maverick politician Dr. Morton Shulman, he made several runs for provincial and civic office. (He once had to be dissuaded from parachuting into Nathan Phillips Square to announce his candidacy.) He also joined the Acres Think Tank, under a fellowship program for five "creative young thinkers," sponsored by the Norman C. Simpson Foundation. At Acres, Norman designed something he called Earth City, a prototype for the development of the Precambrian Shield that included a research college and a Peace Centre. Earth City—based partly on Middle Eastern architectural forms—formed the basis of his graduate architectural thesis but, ahead of its time, it did not meet with favour.

I knew nothing of Earth City, but Norman did discuss with me some of his other Acres ideas. He proposed the construction of a network of riding trails in the Don Valley (ideal, he felt, for handicapped children as well as for tourists). He was also interested in planning integrated old age living and addressing the problems of drug-addicted young people, not a few of whom ended up staying at the three-storey mansion. "The Gallery turned into a hippie haven by accident," he wrote. At one point, a young woman and her small family were living in the basement while various youthful transients crashed upstairs. "I have no interest in being a social worker," Norman said. "But what else can you do? I see them turn from carefree kids into hard-bitten members of a criminal sub-culture. More and more of the kids are turning into speed freaks. But it is hard to get treatment for kids until they are too far gone." Norman even became an advisor to the Ontario Department of Corrections, when his rooming house was designated an official group home—an arrangement that would have ramifications for Norman years in the future.

The Amazon continued to be a prime source of fascination for Norman and he made several expeditions there in the years to come. Some of these were sponsored by the CBC and turned into a film, *Indians of the Upper Amazon*, one of three films he made on native peoples of South America and Papua New Guinea. On one trip, he lost his way in the rain forest, defenceless against prowling jaguars and poisonous snakes; he seemed to take it all in stride. "Some of the best parts of the trips," he said, "are the things that go wrong." He said he learned from his early trips to the Amazon that "you could go into a new society and as long as you are honest and friendly and smile and aren't loud and making them uncomfortable, you'd be accepted." When he heard about a naked jungle tribe who killed outsiders, he determined to disarm them by parachuting into their midst in the nude. As any old-fashioned Imperial adventurer might, he believed that "being a gentleman is the key."

By the early 70's, Norman had established the pattern of living that would last for almost thirty years. He would spend a few months of each year in travels and explorations, the rest at home, writing, painting, fundraising, and hosting visiting potentates like the Emir of Fujairah and the King of Rwanda. Norman used to say he considered his adventures to be both recreations and personal trials, a way to confront his fears. "It's the only way I can keep myself balanced and keep my environment in perspective. When I come back, it makes me appreciate being here in Canada. I put myself in a whole new environment, a whole new dimension, so that when I come back, I find a real refreshment, a real catharsis." In 1972 alone, Norman travelled deep into the New Guinea jungles with his friend Manny Benjamin, took a photography tour of Nepal with his friend Randy Frost, and collected wildlife specimens in Bali. He usually managed to be in Toronto for the annual Royal Winter Fair which he called "the Christmas of my life."

. In the early years of Norman's adventures, he brought back many live "specimens." The return baggage for one trip included nine monkeys, forty snakes, three turtles, four alligators and a vulture. In those days, there were fewer restrictions on the import of such creatures and Norman sold most of the animals to zoos and used the money to finance his trips. A few favourites were given names and kept as pets. Ferrets, pythons (housed in a large herpetarium in the basement and fed on specially prepared mice), monkeys, a tapir, dung beetles, millipedes, fluorescent weevils, hermit crabs, an electric eel, and eventually, lemurs all shared the Bedford Road house which at one point housed about fifty living creatures. For a time, a basement tank housed a big, vicious-looking fish that liked to be fed cherries. "I can't imagine what it would be like not to live with animals," he said when one magazine called him "Toronto's Dr. Doolittle." Two monkeys rescued from Amazonian hunters escaped the house and grounds one day and ended up swinging from nearby trolley-bus wires causing short circuits and "bothersome delays" before they were electrocuted. "With their hair standing on end and a full blast of current racing through them," Norman wrote, "the jungle creatures saved from becoming food died an even more useless death."

The inevitable problems and mishaps—and the progressive tightening of the import rules—ventually convinced him to take a new look at "collecting." "Ten years ago," he told me, "I'd see an animal in the jungle and bring it back. But I'm happy with all the conservation rules in place now, so I don't do that any more. When it comes to wildlife issues, when I have a chance to speak out, I do." He particularly enjoyed taking animals to public schools. One of the most popular guests was Tony, a 300-lb. Galapagos tortoise, a Museum resident for over a decade. At one point an electoral poll at the Museum had to be moved when nervous voters became alarmed as the great creature ambled placidly through the voting booths. (Tony's stuffed remains now have pride of place in a private collection.)

Norman's favourite of all his animals was Henry the Pig, actually an amiable sow whose sad story was one of good intentions gone awry. "I held her on my lap for hours and she quickly gained confidence," Norman wrote in an article in *Toronto Life* in 1971. "At first she drank milk from a bottle, then graduated to commercial 'pig starter' and 'pig grower.' Later I sometimes fetched a bucket of slop for her from a restaurant...Henry's size and affection grew by the day. She liked to jump on the couch when I was resting, nuzzle her way across my chest and lie there. As she approached 200 pounds, this became ludicrous, and my only recourse was to scratch her stomach. A stomach scratch sent Henry into ecstasy. She would immediately roll off the couch onto her back and call for more. She uttered an amazing range of sounds to signify hunger, thirst, leisure, fear, love, anger," and enjoyed playing games with the neighbourhood children.

Henry loved beer which she would cadge from guests. Intelligent and house-trained, she "only had accidents when frightened. Once when we were guests on Elwood Glover's show, I picked her up, which Henry hated; she squealed and forgot herself all over the guest chair on national television." Baths were not enjoyed; her screams could be heard down the block. But most of the time, Norm declared, she complemented what he described as "the informality of my house" with "great good humour and grace."

"Everyone in our house loved Henry, except Herman the Pony and our senior cat. The cat, a tough old matriarch who feared neither man nor dog, tried to bully the pig. Thick-skinned Henry ignored her claws, which freaked the cat out so badly she finally left Henry alone." But Herman the Pony couldn't get along with Henry and had to be returned to his farm—in the back of Norman's beat-up old limousine which caused a police summons for "blocking traffic."

"Henry and I often strolled down Yonge Street," Norman recalled. "People would follow us for blocks. Henry paid little attention until some thoughtful person scratched her stomach, whereupon she instantly rolled onto her back in the middle of the sidewalk...Otherwise she trotted along about ten paces behind me. I never needed a leash. She never dirtied the streets or molested passers-by."

None of Norman's immediate neighbours objected to Henry. But for one woman down the street, the pig's very existence became unbearable. "In the end," Norman lamented, "she brought the overwhelming weight of officialdom down on us." She complained to the alderman, who eventually involved the police, the fire department, the Humane Society, the City Buildings Department, the Health Department, a mortgage company and three insurance companies." Once Norman had to jump out of bed to hide Henry from a particularly officious inspector. Henry dragged Norm, still naked, into the yard while the inspector took notes. On the other side in the pig war, whole school classes wrote letters to the Mayor and the authorities pleading leniency for Henry.

On her premium diet, Henry grew healthy and hearty, eventually topping 300 pounds. One day Norman returned home to find sixteen policemen with six squad cars and two motorcycles in front of the house. Henry had gotten into the street. One cop had her by the tail; another had a coil of rope and a third was threatening to shoot her. "I rushed over, asked them to release her and called her name," Norm wrote in an account of the Henry saga he wrote for *Toronto Life* magazine. "Go indoors!" he told her. She promptly ran into the house. "The police stood around looking formidable and a bit foolish. Some were angry; the rest came in for coffee. One cop warned, 'If I ever see you and that pig on the street again... I'll arrest you.'" Soon afterwards, Norman's house insurance was suddenly cancelled on unspecified "moral grounds." This left the mortgagee free to foreclose on the uninsured mortgage. Norman was in peril of losing his home, but managed to save it at the last minute thanks to some reinsurance through an influential friend.

Over the years Norman and the Bedford Road house came to the attention of the authorities for various misdemeanours including, most memorably, the electrocuted monkeys. But the outrageous presence of Henry the Pig became a particular irritant to local officialdom. In the face of increasing opposition, Henry's supporters bailed out one by one as her enemies grew more determined. Norman came to see the stockyards as the only solution.

"I called Henry from the back yard where she was playing, tossing leaves over herself. She came running. As we went down the lane, I knew she expected to go for another stroll. I opened the car door and she hopped in obediently. As we drove to the stockyards, she put her big head over the seat and rested it trustfully on my shoulder." The carnage at the stockyards panicked Henry and she cowered in a corner as the other pigs butted and sniffed her. Her ear was bitten. "Henry kept looking up at me. I felt it pain-fully." Norman knew she was asking for water but her new owners refused. "I spent hours that night, thinking. Where did my responsibility end? On the day Henry was slaughtered, the inspectors and others who helped drive her to her death still kept coming to the house to look for her. On that same day, I had a meeting with Ontario's deputy minister of correc-tional services to talk about prison and reform schools...I could only think of Henry. Should I have consigned her to the prison of a farm? Was I wrong in permitting her slaughter? I wish now I had tried harder to find an alter-native."

A few years later, Toronto's Riverdale Farm, now a well-run chil-dren's farm with a small number of cattle, horses, goats and chickens might have made a pleasant home for Henry. But in Henry's time, the farm was an overcrowded zoo, and no place for a sensitive pig. Too late, Norman real-ized he had not fought hard enough, and his guilt weighed heavily on him. "She trusted me, and all humanity, and all of us let her down," he wrote. "There is no place in urban officialdom for the nonconformist."

The Henry problem was followed by other run-ins with local authori-ties. At one point Norman rescued a ten-foot high ornamental iron fence that had once kept polar bears in an enclosure. Installed around the front of his property, it made a handsome addition to the site. Unfortunately, it contravened local height restrictions and a neighbour complained. Another protracted struggle ensued. Norman eventually won that one, but the offi-cial files labelled ELDER, NORMAN were growing ever fatter.

Once Norman and I were cruising down Yonge Street in his old car, a former mourner's limousine acquired from a funeral parlour and enhanced with putty and animal bones. I remember that Norman was sporting the excellent toupee he wore only to gala events and parties. We were stopped by the police. Apparently a fringed blind in the back window was obscuring the view from the driver's seat, or so the cop said. Norman amiably agreed to remove the obstruction. "Weren't you on TV?" the cop asked. Once he realized who Norm was, it was all smiles and Norman was let go with a jocular caution. Fortunately, they saw no need to inspect the trunk, as a large reptile was sleeping off a meal in there.

Our leisurely cruise up Yonge Street was halted by a commotion just ahead of us. Norman got out of the car and ran over to a man who had just been hit by a now-stopped vehicle and was lying on the ground moaning. Norman ran over, threw a coat over him - —he appeared to have a broken leg—and by the time the police arrived (which was very quickly as they were nearby stopping miscreants like us) Norman had calmed the accident victim down and the two of them were chuckling together. Norman gave an officer his name and particulars and we went on our way. Then I remem-bered Norman had left his coat behind. "Oh, it doesn't matter," he said. "Even this shirt I'm wearing came from someone's garbage." I remembered his remark that "I always keep one foot in the gutter."

Throughout the 1970's Norman continued his journeys to the jungle.

He returned to the Amazon to collect reptiles for zoos, filmed the isolated people of the remote Buka Buki on the April River in the New Guinea highlands, took a photography tour of the Nepalese mountains and a collecting tour of Bali. He went canoeing on the Onakawana River near James Bay, explored the Florida Everglades, Namibia and the Tierra Del Fuego region in the far south of Argentina.

In 1974, Norman published *The Destructive Will*, a title taken from a quotation by Schopenhauer about the "all-consuming devouring will that creates itself in order to destroy itself." Dedicated to a list of friends, the book consists of a series of free verse meditations accompanied by fantastical, sometimes violent, pen-and-ink sketches resembling Cocteau's drawings under the influence of opium: people jump—and shit—out of windows; a bird is impaled on a weathervane; a naked man with an erection reads to a crowd of rooted heads; long-necked creatures emerge from the belly of a horse with a man's face; a headless corpse dismembers itself with an axe. Friendship and love are contrasted with apocalyptic visions and "blessings too sweet to endure." *The Destructive Will* reveals Norman's hit-and-miss learning; he knew his Schopenhauer but spelled chimpanzee "chimpansey."

At the end of the decade, excerpts from the Amazon notebooks were published in an illustrated edition by Toronto's New Canada Publications as *This Thing of Darkness*, with a Foreword by his old acquaintance, H.R.H.Prince Philip. People often asked how he was able to "get the Duke." Norman said he just wrote to the palace and asked him. Charmingly illustrated with drawings and photographs, this account of journeys to the Marubas and Ticunas is straightforward and poignant, quite different from the elliptical, poetic *Noshitaka* trilogy. The book includes a photo of Norman wrestling a five-metre-long anaconda on a muddy riverbank, and a note about "the almost claustrophobic feeling of being trapped with no escape from paradise."

In a Postscript, Norman recounts the problems that befell the "large menagerie I had saved from the jungle stewpot." Shaking with malaria, he nurses a sick monkey (who shits on him and eventually dies in his arms) and then spends two days of delirium in a Bogota hospital before having to do battle with Customs officials at the Toronto Airport. Homes were eventually found for all the animals, though Victor the Vulture hung around for a while, becoming a picturesque, if unpredictable, TV personality. The tapir went to the Toronto Zoo, but "it took action by the chief of the U.S. Environmental Protection Agency and the Canadian Federal Government to get him there."

Often Norman took one or two companions with him on his travels - usually young men who valued a unique opportunity to see hidden parts of the world. For the rest of the year he made the Museum his home base. It became "a revolving door" for artists and travellers. At one point, several artists were using different parts of the house as studios. Norman lived in the main floor and the basement (where the big snakes were kept in a large, sturdy herpetarium). The top two floors of the house were separated off for

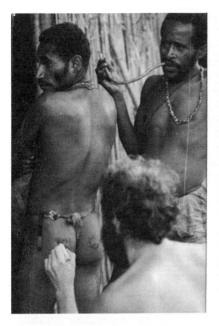

TOP LEFT: The artist at work:
Norman Elder in Papua New
Guinea, 1967.

TOP RIGHT: Noshitaka (privately
printed, 1966), front cover.

LEFT: Lemur with travel journals.
(photo by Norman Elder)

lodgers. Norm always slept late, had breakfast every day at the same restaurant and took everyone's washing to a Chinese laundry on his way to
swim his regular round of laps at the local pool.

The Norman Elder Museum and Gallery became a well known fea-
ture of the area. Its proliferating exhibits (animal specimens, odd artefacts,
Norman's paintings and trophies and an assortment of taxidermal relics
from the Victorian age) provided glimpses of its proprietor's taste in collecting. One visitor, who attended a slide show about Haiti, remembered that
the projector was housed in a baby's coffin. Museum exhibits were frequently rented out as film and theatre props. The interior of the house was
constantly being altered as new artefacts had to be accommodated by additional rooms or knocked-out walls. It was used as a set for countless inex-
pensive horror movies, one TV series, *Robocop*, and one masterpiece, David
Cronenberg's *Naked Lunch* in which the hapless rent-boy Kiki is buggered
by the giant monster in Norman's living room.

The Museum's grounds were modest and well-maintained, not out of
place in the leafy, expensive old neighbourhood. Most of the residents be-
haved themselves. But a house filled with roomers and strangers inevitably
gives rise to strange rumours. There were said to be tunnels somewhere
under the garden. Someone once tried to find one of them and got locked in
a windowless basement room in the dark for over an hour. Once a teenager
dashed into the house carrying a cache of stolen goods. A snake got loose.
A monkey stole a sausage from a neighbour's barbecue. More than once the
police had to be called. But the Museum stayed open to the public (not before 2 PM please). Norman was invariably agreeable and polite, and the
atmosphere at the house tended to be more quiet than rowdy. Any real trou-
blemakers were asked to leave. The press continued to treat Norman kindly,
appreciative of the many good stories he provided. For *Toronto Star* colum-
nist George Gamester in particular, Norman's travels, animals, eccentricities
and remarks were a regular source of good copy, and were amiably reported
with a mixture of condescension and amazement.

Norman also made his own press, writing articles for magazines like
Horse Sport ("Riding in Madagascar"), *The Explorers Journal* ("The Dyaks of
Borneo") and *Doctor's Review* ("Hippo Hunting Hazards"). He played the
part of the Great White Hunter in an insect repellent commercial, exposing
his bare flesh to the hunger of 10,000 blackflies. His "From Pandas to Pen-
guins" presentations at local schools were always a hit.

Hamish Grant was twelve when Norman brought his travelling wildlife show-and-tell to the Grade Six class at Jesse Ketchum Public School. He
began dropping by the Museum and was soon assigned the task of ensuring
that Norman got to his morning school presentations on time. Bypassing a
sign on the front door that said "Do not knock or press buzzer before 2 PM,"
Hamish would bang on a bedroom window to wake him up. "Norm would
come to the front door and let me look around his collection while he got
ready. We'd load a snake or a ferret or a chinchilla into a canvas bag and
head off in one of Norman's cars, stopping off for a donut and coffee on the

way. It was tremendous fun. One time on the way back, I got curious about the day's exhibit, a big jar of thirty live fruit bats." Hamish tried to take one out of the jar but of course "the bats took their cue and exploded out *en masse*, a dark, furry cloud filling the air in the car as we drove along Bloor Street. Norm typically kept his head and pulled the car onto the sidewalk, We spent the next twenty minutes or so climbing all over the interior of the car collecting bats, laughing all the time."

Such mishaps were not untypical. Kevin the Goose and Henry the Pig both disgraced themselves by taking bathroom breaks at inopportune moments on national television. Victor the Vulture did the same while flapping around above the heads of a live studio audience. But to Norman these messy minor mishaps were all part of the jolly fun; they made him laugh. He told me he would like to have taken the animals to hospitals too but of course, it was impossible. He joked about keeping a giraffe in the back yard. "If I get a young one—only twelve feet high—I could train it at Central Don Stables. He'd be comfortable there because he could stand with his head up in the hayloft. Of course I'd have to mount him from a stepladder. I don't know about the reins because the neck is seven feet long. I might have to direct him with feathers attached to the end of a long stick. And if I brought him into the city, he'd have to wear boots because of the hard pavement."

Along with the animals, some of Norman's friends came to live at his house, a few of them after having proved unmanageable elsewhere. Duane Robertson, who would accompany Norman as cameraman on several trips, met him as a teenager at the suburban taping of a TV show. He was causing his mother concern and needed a place to stay. He ended up living at the house until his marriage, twenty years later. As unofficial curator of the Museum, he suggested making it the headquarters of a Canadian chapter of the Explorer's Club in order to encourage more visits by Norman's fellow adventurers. They wrote to all seventy Canadian Explorers Club members, and the Explorers Club of Canada was founded. It is now the largest foreign chapter. Duane's mother believed Norman "saved his life."

"Norm offered opportunities for interesting experiences to a lot of people," Robertson recalled. "He showed me that the world was bigger than Richmond Hill." Long-time friend and house-mate John Haddad said Norman "showed me how to be assertive without being rude." Another acquaintance said simply, "he helped me to grow up."

Norman's travelling companion on his 1982 trip to New Guinea and the Trobriand Islands was not an adventurous young guy with a few free months to spare but Frank Ogden, also known as "Doctor Tomorrow," the eminent author, pilot, LSD researcher and futurist, then 62 years old. The trip proved an unusual one, even for Norman. He and Ogden arrived in the Trobriand Islands at the time of the month-long Yam Festival, which turned out to be something of a local version of Sadie Hawkins Day. "It's really a socially accepted time," Ogden explained, "for the young women of the islands to go out and sexually attack the men in what amounts to gang-rapes." During this popular celebration of predatory sex and lovingly cooked yams, Ogden reminisced, "about 4,000 man-hungry women go on a rampage wearing only coconut oil and tiny loin-cloths." To escape the loud enthusiasm of the local ladies, the two Canadians got lost in the jungle for a few days where they were able to collect specimens of some of the 10,000 different insect species native to the region. Having dodged, more or less, the seasonal yam frenzy, Norman returned to beguile the locals by touching his nose with his tongue and walking on his hands—tricks he found hugely popular in most parts of the world.

Later in the Eighties Norman went to the former Belgian Congo with Robert Cudney and Ralph Reppert, on a journey sponsored by the *Toronto Sun*. "I'm just back from Zaire," Norman wrote, "and I've got a few amoebic parasites in my system. I was living with the pygmies and they kept offering me these live slugs which are a special treat for them. Well, you don't want to hurt their feelings so you have to eat them. But you do get tired of slugs after a while." In Namibia and Botswana, Norman had to be careful not to go into the local villages at night as it was considered impolite to refuse a chief's offer of one of his wives. "The women wash only three times in their lives," Norman noted in one of his many journals, "on their wedding day and with the deaths of their parents."

On another trip, to the interior of Borneo, Ralph Reppert fell into a river and was almost swept away. "The incident made me think of how serious it could be if someone were to get hurt," Norman mused, as though the thought had never occurred to him before. "There are no doctors anywhere in these mountain communities." But Norman—and his companions —always seemed to be lucky—a luck that was often bolstered by considerable help from friendly local missionaries, for whom Norman always expressed great appreciation.

1989 marked Norman's fiftieth birthday. "I am amazed that I ever made it to fifty," he said. "I didn't think that I would come back from all my trips or walk away from all my sky jumps. And now I feel I've got this extra time that I'm not quite sure what to do with." He wondered if he had a death wish, but decided he "didn't want to die." As it happened, he had another fourteen years left to go.

For all his eccentricity and apparent independence, Norman always maintained his ties to his family and the Rosedale horsey set — wealthy, generally conventional people who knew Norman through family or sporting connections. (Norman's brother Jim was also a prize-winning Olympic equestrian and Norman earned extra money by painting portraits of the horses owned by family and friends.) With these relations in mind, he was always discreet about his homosexuality. At a time when gays were ostensibly becoming more accepted, Norman played no apparent role in public gay life. He belonged to no gay community groups, was involved with no gay charities, frequented public swimming pools rather than bathhouses, and avoided not only gay bars but even discretely ambiguous bisexual gathering places. At Gay Pride celebrations, he was absent. He had gay friends among whom he could speak frankly, some of them as closeted as himself.

But to the increasingly visible gay community, he was a stranger. Perhaps like many gay men who had grown up in an era of total illegality, he believed that discretion was the better part of valour.

The social and legal situation for gay men in Canada changed rapidly throughout the 1980's and '90's as the AIDS crisis and a series of hard-fought legal and judicial victories brought new visibility. It was rapidly becoming unacceptable to scorn or persecute gay men as such. But where once group fantasies had been projected upon "homosexuals," now the feared offenders were characterized as a growing army of male "pedophiles." This terminological slight of hand was facilitated by the fact that while being gay had become theoretically acceptable, the Age of Consent for homosexual relations, set at 21 by the Trudeau reforms of 1969, remained in force. Well into the '80's, even sexually mature males of 19 or 20 were said to be legally children, and therefore incapable of consent to homosexual activity. This at a time when increasing numbers of young people were coming out as gay or lesbian, some even forming high school gay clubs and taking same-sex dates to the prom.

Public awareness of past sexual abuses in Canadian orphanages and Native schools increased public anxiety. Old fears began to surface in the form of a series of moral panics involving allegations of manic sexual violence. In one urban centre after another, groups of children were claiming to have been raped, forced to drink blood, consume human body parts and have intercourse with dogs and bats. Babies were said to have been skinned alive and barbecued, or flown to Mars and thrown into schools of sharks. Investigations uncovered no missing infants, the alleged burial sites yielded no remains, and no sharks were located. Nevertheless, several high-profile jury trials resulted in convictions and heavy sentences. Innocent people were jailed, families broken up and lives ruined. Eventually, many of the children involved admitted their lies had been prompted by social workers and court officials and most of the sentences were reversed. Years later, Saskatchewan Justice Minister Frank Quennell lamented this "truly regrettable situation," calling the 1980's and '90's "a unique period in the history of the justice system throughout North America."

In the early '90's, Julian Fantino, the ambitious Chief of Police in London, Ontario, claimed, with much fanfare, to have uncovered a "kiddie sex ring" that turned out to be an unremarkable series of consensual relationships among adult men and a few teenaged hustlers. Again, there was a great deal of damage to lives and reputations; one man committed suicide. Other similar cases followed. It was in this toxic atmosphere that a series of sensational revelations about boys, sex and hockey, was given maximum publicity by the national media during the late 1990's. Sheldon Kennedy, a young hockey player, had revealed that his coach, Graham James, had been having inappropriate relations with some of his young players. The *Globe and Mail* editorialized about "a diseased game." Suddenly, people were asking big questions about the world of junior hockey. Crime writer James Dubro wrote that it seemed as if sex with boys had become "the *crime du jour."*

Soon after the Graham James case broke, Martin (originally Arnold) Kruze, a troubled, sexually confused bankrupt in his mid-thirties, added his own twist to the sports scandals, revealing a series of unsavoury sexual goings-on twenty years in the past at Toronto's famous Maple Leaf Gardens, the nation's premier hockey arena. Two years earlier, Kruze had been paid $60,000 for an "agreement of silence" about the repeated sexual abuse he said he had suffered as a boy at the hands of low-level Gardens employees. The Criminal Injuries Compensation Board awarded him another $22,000.

The Gardens had traditionally been run with quasi-military punctilio, but with the advent of the Harold Ballard regime in 1972, "everything went to rat-shit" because, as one former employee put it, "the new employees were a bunch of pirates." Under "Pal Hal," Gardens staff were often left unsupervised. Several men on the staff began using games tickets and other favours to entice young boys to have sex with them and with selected girls. As oversight declined at the Gardens, revenue plunged, and the impulsive Ballard decided more seats were the answer. The iconic half-century old gondola from which Foster Hewitt had called every game was unceremoniously torn out and thrown into the incinerator. Ballard's action was solemnly denounced by *The Toronto Star* as "the barbaric destruction of one of Canada's great cultural monuments." When Ballard heard this —an employee read it to him—he is said to have exploded in paroxysms of rage and hilarity, choking on his cigar and sending a shower of ash across the accumulated detritus of his desk. Ballard was eventually convicted of 47 counts of theft, fraud and tax evasion and sent to an institution he laughingly described as a country club, where he was allowed to drink beer with the guards.

By 1997, Ballard had been dead for several years and the Gardens was about to be squabbled over as an immensely valuable piece of Toronto real estate. With the Graham James case already engaging the media, Martin Kruze decided to renounce his previous vow of silence and go public with claims of abuse. News programs publicized his charges and the Maple Leaf Gardens scandal became a huge story of its own. In a letter to the media about the case, Kruze alleged that he had been taken advantage of not merely by a few hired maintenance men but by an organized "ring" that decades later was still operating at the Gardens. Kruze, who had begun to describe himself as "an innocent child of God," rapidly became a professional survivor (he even had a calling card printed with SURVIVOR on it). Ostensibly heterosexual, with an official girlfriend, he admitted he was still having sex with men, claiming he did it to punish himself for past misdeeds. He had become part of what he called "the sexual abuse industry." When asked by one reporter if he was a blackmailer, he referred any such discussion to his attorney.

Toronto Sun editor Lorrie Goldstein admitted later that the subsequent press and television coverage of the sordid Maple Leaf Gardens case was largely driven by homophobia. One veteran police detective who worked the case tried to tell the media there was no truth to the claims of a wide-ranging "pedophile ring" responsible even for a notorious 1977 child murder. But the lack of a "ring," he said, "spoils their whole story....The whole thing about this sex ring grew and grew." As a result, the Toronto police force was under great pressure to uncover more participants in the elusive ring. After Detective Dan Tredrea, chief investigator on the case, went on the six o'clock news asking for more victims to come forward, the phones, said one officer, began "ringing off the hook...It's been dozens and dozens, literally." One complainant claimed to have been molested "about fifty times," and to have told no one. More men who had known the accused Gardens employees (there were three, one of them deceased) presented themselves to the police. As no sex ring could be substantiated and no Gardens officials could be implicated, the men were pressed to remember names from further afield. One name that came up repeatedly was that of Norman Elder, and the police were able to produce a fat file of past misdemeanours and complaints, including the trolley-fried monkeys, the big pig and the polar bear fence, as well as the names of various reform school graduates who had dallied at the house.

Martin Kruze's sensational revelations about pederastic goings-on in our national sport's most sacred site were inevitably discussed in taverns and coffee-shops across the country, often in tandem with the enviable sum he had been paid to keep quiet. And it set in motion a chain of events that led to the first of a dozen serious criminal charges against Norman Elder. Norman had no connection to Maple Leaf Gardens or its employees, and no interest in the young boys involved. But several of the boys had later met Norman, and knew he was gay. His house was only a few hundred yards from Varsity Stadium, the main sports field at the University of Toronto. Of an evening, Norman would often stroll down to catch a game. He would fall into conversation with other spectators, sometimes inviting them to make the short trip home with him. Some enjoyed a cup of tea and a tour of the Museum. Others stayed the night. And back in the '70's, what occasionally ensued afterwards was deemed criminal if one or both parties were shy of the legal age of 21.

While the police began to prepare their case against Norman, there were ominous developments even closer to home. A one-time Bedford Road resident, a mentally disturbed man with a penchant for petty theft, had at one time become involved with a friend of Norman's called Steve, the putative heir to a well-known Canadian food chain. The relationship had worked out badly, the young thief had been asked to leave the house and had later come to the notice of the police. He blamed Steve, and secondarily Norman for his troubles, and when he read about the Maple Leaf Gardens case, he and a friend began to discuss the possibilities of blackmail. One evening, they phoned the Norman Elder Museum and Gallery, looking for Steve, or at least his phone number. None too happy to hear from the pair, Norman told them the facts: "You're too late. Steve's dead.   He died of a massive

aneurism in Belize a few months ago." Shortly after that call, Norm began
confiding to a few close friends that an acquaintance was trying to blackmail him, and that he was neither willing nor able to pay. Before the year
was out, Norman was arrested.

Hundreds of people had stayed at the Museum in the decades since
the move from Yorkville. Many of his friends and protégés had now become
established citizens with families, jobs, businesses or professional lives.
But others had become petty criminals, hustlers or perennial bankrupts. It
was this second group that provided most of the ten men who now revealed
to the police that Norman had initiated sex with them up to a quarter of a
century earlier.

After the shock of his initial arrest, Norman realized he would have
to decide quickly on a course of action. The question was: whether to con-
test the charges in court, or to fold and hope his exemplary record and establishment connections would outweigh the flawed recollections and con-
tradictory contentions of an apparently growing list of accusers. "Dr. Tomorrow," Norman's old friend Frank Ogden, strongly urged him to plead
Not Guilty and fight. One of Canada's best-known criminal lawyers was
mentioned as a possible counsel. The substantial fees involved might have
presented a problem, but there were several able local lawyers who could
have taken the case, including one whose unofficial office was a window
booth in a Yonge Street fast food restaurant, from which perch he had become a shrewd observer of the very world in which Norman's accusers
moved. Others of riper vintage retained their ancient knowledge of those
obsolete sections of the Criminal Code under which Norman had been
charged. Family members on the other hand dreaded what promised to be a
long and gruelling trial with much attendant publicity and embarrassing
unpleasantness. Norman decided to avoid further disgrace by signing a
court document known as an "Agreed Statement of Facts," otherwise referred to in the business as a confession. As his solicitor he retained a
young attorney with connections to the Elder family. Norman's arrest was
kept quiet; many of his friends heard nothing about it. Nevertheless, the
word was soon out on the street. Men whom Norman had bailed out of jail
decades before suddenly remembered him—the guy with the weird house on
Bedford Road who took them water-skiing, or offered them cash for a blow
job, or let them crash in his upstairs and took care of their laundry.

In October of 1997, I answered Norman's request for a letter of
reference to present to the court. His attorney amassed fifty-eight of these,
all from people who knew him, including an impressive number of well-
known and distinguished names. They described Norman in "the highest
possible terms," the court agreed, "and as a valued and highly respected
member of the community." Many of the letters attested to Norman's taking
in "confused and lost" young—and not-so-young—people, helping them, re-
establishing contact with their families and setting them on the path to
"productive lives." His trial began in January, 1998, with the prosecutor
asking Judge Faith Finnestad to give "minimum weight" to any letters at-

testing to the defendant's good character on the grounds that his supporters were obviously "not aware that this aspect of his personality existed." Against the stack of character references were the sworn statements of ten accusers. The men, all sexually mature males at the time of the alleged events and now approaching middle age, were seen by the court as having been children in the eyes of the law, and thus incapable of consent. Under the statutes in force in the early '70's, no force or even coercion needed to be alleged; a mere sexual advance was an illegal act. One man said that when Norman had "gotten on top of him," he had "got up and prepared to leave the premises." After calming him, intercourse was attempted but "no penetration took place." "At the present time," he wrote, "I fantasize...that I will stop having the nightmare of being chased by an old male."

In a brief address to the court, Norman admitted he had broken the law, apologized for the distress he had caused and added that "it's been very difficult for my friends, my family and myself." Nonetheless, the prosecutor demanded jail time, stressing the large number of offences and characterizing the defendant as "a predator" who had "ensnared vulnerable youth." Sympathetic observers heard echoes of the notorious summing-up by Mr. Justice Wills in the Oscar Wilde case a century earlier, when he remarked from the bench that "you, Wilde, have been the centre of a circle of extensive corruption of the most hideous kind among young men." On March 12, Judge Finnestad handed down a sentence of two years less a day, to be served in a provincial prison. Disheartened, Norman instructed his attorney to appeal; he was freed until the appeal was heard. Two weeks later, the police laid two additional charges against him, to be tried, together, the following January.

The following ten months were difficult ones for Norman and friends saw little of him. Though he had always enjoyed reasonably good health, his sleep patterns had become increasingly disturbed, perhaps aggravated by the "listlessness" that sometimes accompanies recurrent malaria. A physician who had been close to Norman's deceased parents began prescribing the drug Ativan, a powerful soporific and anti-depressant. He began taking the drug regularly, and came to rely on it to get to sleep.

In January of 1999, Norman faced his second major court appearance. Stunned by his failure to avoid a jail sentence in the first, uncontested, trial, he had decided to fight the additional accusations, which were made by two men he knew well but who by court order could not be identified. He pleaded Not Guilty to indecently assaulting the first complainant in 1979 and 1980 and the second in 1989. Both men alleged that Norman had performed oral sex on them. One claimed that Norman had once gotten him drunk in Muskoka. Norman was able to show that the beer was bought by the complainant. The man's long history of alcoholism, drug abuse, theft and domestic violence tended to cast further doubts on his veracity, as did his pressing financial troubles and threats of lawsuits. The second man claimed Norman had paid him twice, for sex, and said he had kept the proffered $200. But there were a number of serious inconsistencies in his testimony.

Mr. Justice David McCombs pointed out that the Crown's case relied wholly on the claims of these two witnesses, both of them silent for twenty years. He found their testimony neither credible nor reliable. "However morally repugnant the conduct of Mr. Elder may be," he said, "I am not convinced the acts were criminal...I do not know where the truth lies, so I therefore find Mr. Elder not guilty on both counts." One of the ten accusers in the earlier case was in court for the verdict. Indignant, he told the press, "This man is a legendary pee-dophile" who should be forced to "take treatment." He and the others were having a victims' meeting that very afternoon, he said, to discuss civil action.

A few days after the acquittal, an old friend of Norman's held a quiet dinner party at his Rosedale apartment to celebrate the acquittal. The guests included historian Don McLeod, crime writer James Dubro and playwright Sky Gilbert; Norman was the guest of honour. The host was John Grube who had taught the adolescent Norman years before at Upper Canada College where he remembered Norman as a quiet, personable athlete. A writer, artist and translator, Grube was the author of a fictional treatment of the notorious 1981 Toronto bathhouse raids which galvanized the gay community to mass civil disobedience. He had been close to Jacques Ferron, the Quebec novelist and doctor to the poor who later founded the Rhinocerous Party.

The old professor was silver-haired now and beginning to grow frail, but had lost none of his radical fire. Over after-dinner drinks, he mounted a forceful argument for a rallying of public opinion against Norman's sentence. The testimony of fifty-eight citizens might have been set aside, but maybe the outrage of fifty-eight hundred could make the difference between prison and freedom. Norman sipped his brandy and appeared unconvinced. Shy of further publicity, he suggested his establishment connections would see him through in the end. One guest, a young friend of Grube's whispered, "Who does he know? Conrad Black?"

Don McLeod recalled meeting Norman at the party. He found him charming but "a bit befuddled or dazed" by his trials. "I remember clearly," he recalled, "that he didn't even remember some of the young men who brought the charges against him. I think he was optimistic that the verdict (in the first trial) would be overturned on appeal. At the end of the evening, Norman drove us all home in the snow in his big Lincoln. We briefly got lost trying to find our way out of Rosedale."

The next month, Norman's appeal was denied and he began his two year sentence in a minimum security jail near Brampton, Ontario. In May, his accusers filed a four million dollar lawsuit. Perhaps they believed Norman to be wealthy. In fact, he had almost no money, his house and car were mortgaged, and his only assets were the various records of his travels and a ramshackle cottage in Torrance, Ontario.

In September, Norman wrote to me from prison: "Great to hear from you! It is very easy to feel very cut off when in jail. So it means a lot getting your letter." He mentioned John Grube's much-appreciated dinner party. Jail, he said, "has truly been an interesting experience, with each day a challenge to see if I can make the adjustment to a world that is definitely harder for me than any of my travels into the rainforests. I do like to pretend I'm in a different sort of adventure here. I keep busy reading, drawing, keeping fit and working in the craft shop. Everyone here has been respectful including all the staff." He mentioned that he still had the books I'd given him over the years—at home of course; he was allowed no outside literature. To another friend, he mentioned the pleasure he took in preparing the hot rocks the Native prisoners used for their sweat lodges.

I visited Norman soon after his release, several months ahead of schedule. Sitting in his old bedroom, glad to be back in familiar surroundings, he was relieved that he had at least been able to keep his property and belongings. He looked well and seemed eager to get on with life. The following January, I invited him to attend a literary party at the Idler Pub, just around the corner from his house. It was a chilly night; the occasion was a memorial get-together to commemorate the life of the poet Edward Lacey, who had died in a Toronto rooming house in 1995. Norman was in good spirits. It was the last time I saw him.

Soon after the Lacey memorial, Norman began hearing rumours of possible further police action against him. In addition, the four million dollar lawsuit was making its way through the court system, and he again faced the prospect of losing virtually everything he owned. Understandably, he became somewhat paranoid, fearing every knock on the door. For some time, Norman had been taking Ativan, a strong benzodiazopine tranquillizer misprescribed to him for his persistent insomnia. Ativan is a problematic drug. Its side effects can include "agitation, anxiety, depression, persistent and unpleasant memories and a feeling of unreality." Nightmares, paranoia and panic attacks are not uncommon. At around the time of the Idler gathering, Norman's prescription for the drug had been suddenly cut off. Ativan is highly addictive and can require regular increases in dosage to achieve the required effect. Going off the drug without a carefully supervised program of withdrawal can lead to mental disorientation and suicidal thoughts. Sleepless and agitated, Norman began buying it occasionally on the black market. The disorientation brought about by Ativan probably intensified an already anxious mental state. His worries about his precarious financial situation and the ongoing civil suit began to prey on his mind. He feared being arrested again, and imagined being left destitute.

One day in October of 2003, a friend accompanied Norman to a meeting at the home of an Elder family member. Hoping for a loan on generous terms that would at least meet his ongoing expenses, he asked his friend to wait for him in the car while he went inside. When he returned, he looked shaken: no loan would be forthcoming. At about this time, he phoned his friend, Bill Jamieson, a fellow Explorers Club member. Jamieson was a dealer in rare tribal artefacts who had purchased the contents of the old Niagara Falls Museum, storing some of the former exhibits at Norman's house. Norman told Jamieson he was going to sell the building; would he please come and remove his belongings? Jamieson suggested he could tide Norman over with a loan; Norman thanked him but declined the offer.

That evening or the next, John Haddad, the friend who shared Norman's part of the house, cooked Norman his favourite meal of bacon and eggs. As they sat together in the rudimentary kitchen, the cupboard door immediately opposite Norman, which a slight tilt to the floor invariably kept shut, slowly swung wide open. John Haddad made a comment about omens. Norman smiled but said nothing.

The following morning, John Haddad was puzzled to find the pet lemurs Norman had brought back from Madagascar had not been fed. Shortly afterwards on his return from a shopping trip, Haddad found one of the lemurs in a highly agitated state, jumping back and forth onto a day-bed in Norman's room. When he went into the bedroom to sit on the day-bed and find out what the lemur wanted, he saw Norman's body, hanging lifeless from a fixture in the ceiling. In one of those visual hallucinations a sudden shock can induce, the corpse appeared eerily, impossibly small. Police and ambulance were summoned. As a pair of paramedics eased the body down, one of them remarked to the other, "He's in pretty good shape."

Seven squad cars quickly descended on 140 Bedford Road and for the last time, official investigators ranged over the premises, taking note of the excited lemurs and curiously decorated coffins, and stringing crime scene tape around the perimeter. For years there had been rumours that tunnels had been dug under the property. Some people had discerned a resemblance between Norman and the actor Bob Crane who played Col. Hogan in the '80's TV show *Hogan's Heroes*, set in a World War II prisoner-of-war camp. Now, Toronto's Finest were convinced that Norman's bed, like the trick bunk in Hogan's barracks, must be the concealed entrance to a tunnel or system of tunnels leading to an outbuilding, or to the house next door, or even under the street to a manhole cover serving as an escape hatch. Seismic equipment was brought in, revealing no secret passages, only Norman's windowless "funky room" in the cellar and a false door fastened to one of the walls. Nothing was found in the garden but a few old lion bones.

Shortly after Norman's death, Duane Robertson had a dream of his old friend hoisting a cup of coffee, saying "I'm not afraid now."

There seems little doubt that Norman committed some of the acts with which he was charged. He propositioned, and sometimes had sex with, young men, at a time when Canadian law made such activity illegal. But in writing this piece, I spoke with a number of men who in their youth had lived or travelled with Norman. Without exception, the heterosexual ones, some now married and with families, said Norman had never even made a pass at them. One man said, "I've slept in beds and hammocks with Norman and he never did *anything*." They were surprised to hear of Norman's arrest and did not believe the charges against him. But a gay man who had known Norman, a retired civil servant who lived briefly at the Bedford Road house as a long-haired hippie youth, remembered Norman offering a reduction of his already low rent should a bit of sex be involved. As he didn't fancy Norman and was not in the prostitution business, he declined the offer and no more was said about it. He didn't believe the charges either.

It might seem odd that though the young men Norman was accused of assaulting were said to have "immediately fled under cover of darkness," in the court's somewhat melodramatic phrase, he nonetheless continued the unsuccessful seduction technique of suddenly appearing in his victims' beds. Perhaps, like the man who picked up women at bus stops, he was often met with outrage but was pleased to get quite a few takers as well. Still, the stories of innocent youths assaulted as they slept do not seem to square with accounts of gentlemanly behaviour in other, similar circumstances. But there may be a relatively simple explanation.

For bisexual men, uncomfortable with their own capacity to be aroused in the presence of another male, compromising situations have traditionally been explained away by pleading a) I was asleep through the whole thing, b) I was so drunk I didn't know what I was doing, or c) I did it for the money. All these explanations were used by witnesses against Norman. One accuser said "I told him to stop but he said, 'Go back to sleep, don't worry.' He performed fellatio for a half-hour." Another claimed, falsely, that Norman had gotten him drunk. Others admitted they were aroused, and paid. Though Norman's gaydar seems to have been in good working order, his courtship techniques might have benefited from a little polish. Whether his actions merited a prison sentence so many years after the fact is debatable.

It was not long before members of Norman's family removed the furnishings and other useable items from the house. Most of Norman's paintings were auctioned off in lots along with the rest of the contents, including items Norman had borrowed or was storing for friends. One collector remembers seeing some of his own property at an antique stall, acquired from Norman's estate as one of a large number of lots. On Bedford Road, dumpsters rapidly filled up with bug-ridden crocodile parts and moth-eaten stuffed sheep. John Haddad and the remaining lodgers moved out and the house interior was gutted. The polar bear fence and the stone memorial for Jim Butcher, an old friend of Norman's who had died young, were all hauled away, just as many of the tribal cultures Norman had visited were being swept aside by bulldozers and factory farms. Today, the house at 140 Bedford Road bears no trace of what for thirty-five years had been the Norman Elder Museum and Gallery.

Though he seemed utterly at home in the Toronto of the late Twentieth Century, Norman Elder resembled nothing so much as an English gentleman adventurer of the Edwardian era, his cabinet of curiosities enlarged into a private museum with trophies mounted on its walls and curious creatures taking over the anteroom. Like any number of Edwardian gentlemen, Norman appeared to be wealthy but in fact was not. He was an eccentric who insisted, "Norman is *normal*," his use of the third person distancing him from his own ingenuous claim.

Norman was one of those people who always seem faintly amused by life. Once, just for fun at a fancy Toronto party, he placed a enormous, somnolent snake beneath a warm pile of coats on a bed. As the affair wound down and the dowagers were retrieving their wraps, a sudden shriek made everyone jump: Toronto the Good—*meet the jungle!* Though there was no malice in these childish pranks, they could be disturbing, especially after a few drinks. But it *was* a party to remember.

To the end of his life, Norman retained a certain boyishness of appearance and temperament—"running around like a little kid." Hamish Grant said of him that he had something of a Curious George attitude to life. Though he loved an emir or an exiled king, he pretty much took everyone as he found them. Whoever you were, he was invariably interested in what you were up to, and greeted any piece of knowledge sent his way as a revelation, what someone called his "Gee, golly!" approach—Curious George having just found the banana. As with most trusting, good-natured people, Norman often appeared naive. He had seen hunters shoot howler monkeys out of the trees and eat them, yet was shocked by conditions in the local stockyards. He continually confronted the world's destructive will, the "fearful carnivorous god," the anaconda you wrestle for the camera, that almost drowns you. Yet an English poet, who had once fallen into a drunken sleep on Norman's couch over forty years before, remembered him as "one of the calmest and most quietly civilized characters I am likely to meet." He could do extraordinary things on a shoestring, just by being "polite but assertive."

Norman Elder is buried in Torrance, Ontario, near his old cottage. His tombstone describes him as "Explorer, Equestrian, Author and Adventurer." On the grounds of the cottage is an animal graveyard. No one who saw Norman with any of his animals could doubt his affection for them. Here their graves are arranged in neat rows, each with its own individual, sometimes highly idiosyncratic, marker. The cottage and its home-made out-buildings are now falling into desuetude. The cemetery is still maintained by John Haddad.

The Bedford Road house, gutted and up for sale. May 30, 2004.
(photo by Hamish Grant)

Books by Scott Symons (1933 - 2009)

Combat Journal for Place d'Armes: A Personal Narrative.
Toronto, McClelland & Stewart, 1967.
Civic Square. Toronto, McClelland & Stewart, 1969.
Heritage: A Romantic Look at Early Canadian Furniture.
Toronto, McClelland & Stewart, 1973.
Helmet of Flesh. Toronto, McClelland & Stewart, 1986.
Dear Reader: Selected Scott Symons, ed. Christopher Elson.
Toronto, Gutter Press, 1998.

Books by Robin Hardy (1964-2001)

The Day the Homos Disappeared.
     North Vancouver, Gallerie Publications, n.d.
Call of the Wendigo. NY, Bantam Books, 1994.
The Crisis of Desire: AIDS and the Fate of Gay Brotherhood
(with David Groff). Boston, Houghton Mifflin, 1999.

Books by Norman Elder (1939-2003)

Noshitaka. [Toronto], privately printed, 1966.
Oksitartok. [Toronto], privately printed, 1967.
Cannibalistic Catharsis. [Toronto], privately printed, 1969.
The Destructive Will. [Toronto], privately printed, n.d.
This Thing of Darkness: Elder's Amazon Notebooks.
     Toronto, New Canada Publications, 1979.
Norman Elder's Horse Book: Introduction to Riding.
     Toronto, New Canada Publications, 1982.

Also available from Sykes Press:

Delicious
A Memoir of Glenway Wescott
by Daniel Diamond

*D*elicious is an affectionate recollection of the writer Glenway Wescott, author of the classic American novels *The Grandmothers* and *The Pilgrim Hawk*. Poet and painter Daniel Diamond, Wescott's secretary and assistant, provides an intimate, sometimes humorous look at Wescott in his last years — his daily affairs, his writing and opinions, his friendships, his involvement with literary society, and his relationship with his partner, curator Monroe Wheeler. A vivid, uniquely personal view of an important writer whose work is now enjoying a posthumous renaissance.

"The most beautiful piece ever written on Glenway Wescott."
 - Jerry Rosco, author of *Glenway Wescott Personally*

"Totally charming!"
 - Don McLeod, author of *A Brief History of GAY*

"Wonderful — a gem of a gift! I picked it up and read it in a single gulp."
 - Thomas Meyer, author of *At Dusk Iridescent*

"Fascinating!"
 - Timothy d'Arch Smith, author of *The Books of the Beast*

"Very classy, very sweet! Makes me want to write a memoir…oh, that's right, I already did…"
 - Gavin Dillard, author of *In the Flesh*